Deception
Shadows of truth

Timothy J. Amdahl

DEDICATION

I dedicate this book to the true Americans that still believe in their country as I do. To the millions that wish to be heard and are often ignored. I want to thank all those that have served in our armed forces and were willing to put their lives on the line for the rest of us, thank you.

I hope you will enjoy reading this book and hope like my other books, that you will gain insight and knowledge that maybe you were unaware of.

CONTENTS

ACKNOWLEDGMENTS

Welcome to the world of deception, here between the pages of time, we will try and discover the truth, or at least a shadow of the truth. I am just one American who sits and listens to the media present the news, so as to inform us of what is going on. This is why I am presenting this book.

I want to know what is real and what is fake. I want to know who is speaking from the heart and who is speaking from a script. I want America to be run by Americans and not some elite organization from Washington, DC. with hidden agendas.

Follow these stories as they bring out questions that lead us to believe in conspiracies, cover-ups, and deception. Shadows of truth is just a fancy way of not telling the whole truth.

SANDY HOOK

On December 14, 2012 in a small town known as Newtown, Connecticut, a young man known as Adam Lanza would forever leave his legacy in what would be seen as one of the most horrific scenes and schemes of violence, leaving twenty six dead. All but six were children.

Before he arrived at the Newtown elementary school, he shot and killed his mother Nancy Lanza in their home. The news quickly erupted all over. CNN, just one of the many agencies reported, "Just coming across the wires here, a shooting at Newtown Connecticut elementary school. Unsure if there are any victims at this time, but anytime there is word of a shooting, a gun, or shots fired at a school or university, that's just what we do. We will try to keep you updated to the latest."

It is a sad day to know that any person is harmed, let alone a child. In this case twenty children and six adults who never asked to be a part of any cause, or statistic.

They reported on the news, at least twenty seven shot and killed, as they repeat this over and over. They reported the children were told to grab a buddy and walk not run over to the fire station. The parents would be notified and were to meet the children at the fire station. The twenty seventh victim, was found to be Adam Lanza, the shooter. The news continued to grow more and more on this horrific event, as more evidence and information was being brought to light.

What is interesting is all the doubt in this travesty. The news media was not identified in the video clip I just watched, but they were quick to ask questions to the neighbor lady who didn't have a lot of answers. She didn't appear to speculate, or try to make a statement to fit any particular agenda.

The news media, however was quick to focus on the guns rather than the cause when asking questions. The Connecticut State police press conference, was also interesting. The officer stated that the entire area had been searched and absolutely nothing left unturned. Brothers Mark and John Tambascio were owners of the *My Place Bar*. In an interview with one of them they were describing Adam as very fidgety, saying "he couldn't make eye contact." As you watch the interview you see him smirk. I have to ask why is he smirking during an interview that involves so many people dying?

If we go back to the Connecticut State police, more video comes up on the officer prior to the conference, which only adds to more doubt and speculations.

The officer is observed on video saying, "I'm going to promote it, hope it's a sold out show, but don't want anyone's expectations to be too high as to what my performance will be." This statement was made by the same State police officer that held the conference.

The interviewer asked if he could give a step or two, he laughed and stated "No my managers said I can't do that till the night of the performance." It is interesting he sees this as a performance? If this is a performance by an officer of the law, then you might ask how much more is staged and why?

As I started investigating I found interesting video clips that showed people that appeared to be actors playing innocent bystanders or friends or family members of those that were in the midst of a crisis situation. Some of these actors appeared to be the same actors playing multiple roles in different crisis. There was the Guy who states he is Michael Foley, James Foley's brother. In another clip he is Mr. Rohrs and he is holding a baby that too appears to be fake. The lips never move and they show multiple angles only confirming that suspicion even more.

I think When you look at all the news and all the people involved you have to ask how could they do this with such a mass amount of people. How much influence does the media have in reporting the truth rather than fabricate the fake? Are they doing it for ratings and money, or for a more political agenda, such as gun control?

Chloe Anderson admits to using one of these videos to help promote her modeling career.

There is the interview with eight year old Alexis Wasik and her parents that was filmed two days after the Sandy Hook shooting and after watching it many, many times on YouTube it is definitely mind boggling as they point out the bizarre behaviors of the parents, as they appear to hold their child tightly and constantly petting her as to make her aware of their close proximity. As you watch the parents closely you see the dad give the mom eye contact that seems suspicious.

The young girl Alexis is trying to pull her dads hand away from her throat as he holds on tighter. The mom uses her hand to get him to let up a little. It is here that he looks at her and switches hands to make sure he doesn't lose total control.

There are videos that also show that some of these people who appear at one emergency are not the same people that appear at another, or at least that is what the video wants you to think. You do have to ask yourself, if they created this whole façade, would they not create people to go after those that challenge this whole theatrical arena trying to expose them and take the focus back off them?

Before the Sandy Hook incident Newtown, Connecticut was known more for the hospital called Fairfield Hills, which operated from 1931 to 1995 on three hundred acres. It was a hospital that had taken care of the mentally ill and criminally insane.

Connected by tunnels to sixteen red brick buildings where experiments involving electric shock therapy, hydro therapy and frontal lobotomy were done. Mysterious deaths and suicides were also connected to this facility. Because of its haunting setting, the television series *Fear* used its setting in one of its episodes. The movie *Sleepers*, with Robert De Niro was done there as well.

When I was looking around the internet I found a video clip by Broken String Productions that shows an amazing look alike for Alexis Wasik by a girl named Aubrey K. Miller. Who is a young actress and her voice to me, sounds the same as Alexis. It could be just a coincidence, but one interview with Alexis shows her as very outgoing cheerful and not camera shy, while in the other video two days later shows quite the opposite as she is frowning and appears to want to speak but appears fearful and unsure who to trust. When you look at the parents who constantly are touching her to make her aware of their presence makes you wonder what else is going on, or they're hiding?

If we look at Sandy Hook as a crime scene you have to look at everyone as suspects, it only makes sense as we do not want to let any evidence slip by. If we follow Nancy Lanza as a victim we see red flags popping up all over the place. Who is she and what part did she play in the school shooting?

She supposedly is described by some as a teacher, then substitute teacher, and teacher's aide. She is a teacher of special need students that go to the Sandy Hook school.

Nancy Lanza was also married to a man named Peter. There was a teacher that was asked if she knew Nancy Lanza, her name was Abbey Clements, she said she didn't know the last name. I think that statement by itself seems odd, as most teachers run in tight groups at all schools nationwide. What makes sense is that maybe the teacher might have known her under another name such as Annie Haddad. When you look at both Annie and Nancy they looked identical. Maybe because, they were the same person?

What is interesting about Annie is she too taught special needs there and had a student and looked like Nancy and was married to a man whose name too was Peter. They lived less than a mile apart from each other and traveled the same routes. Both women attended monthly mom night outs. Yet no one had ever seen them together at these meetings, or at the school at the same time?

If you look at the interview of the Soto family the children all were smiling with no sign of anger, sadness, or confusion, their sister was killed and yet they talk about her with total control and smiles as one giggles about the snow and sleet being their sister. Later you see on television a show about gun control and all of a sudden it's hard to speak and she points out there is no place in civilian life for an AR- assault rifle. That the weapon left baseball size holes in her sisters clothes that she saw. She states "personally we haven't seen any of the crime scene photos." How is she able to have seen her sisters clothes? Where was she at, when she saw them and would not the area have been locked down and secured?

She states the youngest boy Noah was shot eleven times, as they focus on large capacity guns. She was more emotional talking about guns than she was her sister.

Let us look at Mr. Robbie Parker, Emilie's father who is caught on the news camera actually before he was ready, as he is smiling and laughing having a good time. Here his six year old daughter is killed gun down violently, and he is smiling? In the video he tries to create tears and put on a persona of great emotional atrocity as he stands in front of the camera, yet he wishes to offer his condolences to not just the other victims families, but the shooters family as well? This is one day after the killing of his daughter. He stated the night before he spoke at the church special meeting? The same day his child was killed? He lived in Sandy Hook eight months and has since vanished?

If we look at Gene Rosen who became one of the focal points during the interviews. He was praised for saving and comforting some of the children, but the more we got to know him the more people doubted his entire story. Listening to Gene on one interview he said. "I thought I heard some gunshots, sometimes I hear deer hunters there shots were boom, boom with a pause between them, but these shots were like rapid shots that went very quick, boom, boom, boom."

The news reported that he took in many of the sandy hook children, which we find to then be only four out of seven hundred that went to that school? He took them in giving them stuffed animals and juice only then did he find out what happened and what they had been through according to FOX News.

You need to keep in mind that Gene Rosen is experienced in acting and is the CEO of Newtown Cable Advisory Council. He has appeared in several stage productions such as the Fantastic's. His story constantly changes on how he found the children.

One of the interviews he states he found the kids as he came out of the loft where he fed the cats, another one he was on his way to breakfast, then on one interview he said he saw the children through his window and finally he said he was walking home from breakfast and saw the children on his front lawn. There is the man Gene refers to talking kind of harshly to the children. On another video clip there is a woman guarding them? In some interviews he omits the man who is speaking kind of harshly to the children. He states he heard him say it's going to be alright, it's going to be alright, another one he says he hears him say it's going to be ok, it's going to be ok? How do you say those words harshly?

He stated there was a school bus driver with the kids and he invited them into his house. Would not the school bus driver inform him of what was going on? He stated he saw the six children and thought they were practicing a play or cub scouts? Were all these kids boys? Why would they be in his yard in the first place especially if they were practicing a play or cub scouts? Gene stated there were four boys and two girls, when the bus driver stated there were only four children.

He talks about what the children said, "We can't go back to the school, we can't go back to the school cause we don't have a teacher." He states, "I did not say anything. They just kept telling their story."

"Our teacher is dead. How can we go back we don't have a teacher." He said they kept talking about guns saying he had a big gun and a small gun. Then they talked about blood and said her name, referring to Ms. Soto the 27 year old teacher.

Here is another question, was Gene Rosen married? Does he have kids or grandchildren? If no why would he have stuffed animals in his house? There is a picture showing stuffed animals as though it was a staged photo. Why would you offer juice and stuffed animals in the first place? Gene was a former psychologist who had worked at the Fairfield Hills hospital, if we remember treated the mentally ill and criminally insane.

The school bus driver had the presence of mind to call his supervisor who must have had a contact list, so says Gene Rosen. Yet the school bus driver never had the presence of mind to bring it to Gene's attention upon being invited in to his house, instead he has to wait for the kids to tell him what happened fifteen, twenty minutes later? To me this is all so strange.

Gene stated he took the kids to the fire house. On one occasion he stated all the parents picked up the kids. The official report supposedly states that three children were picked up at Gene Rosen's house while the fourth kid was taken by both to the fire house. Gene mentions after the kids were picked up meeting with a woman by the name Scarlet Lewis, who is the mother of Jessie, who is another hero. Jessie was not just a victim but a hero as Jessie told the others to run while Adam was reloading his magazine.

The whole story is then debunked as video appears showing Gene walking around at the school at 10:30 am outside in the parking lot. He even did an interview at that time supposedly.

Lexxtext 526 Sandy Hook Video on YouTube, points out some interesting facts or assumptions, let's look at them and see where it may lead. Victoria Soto's Face book page was created four days prior to the shooting, on December 10,2012. Looking at the page you can see the date clearly. After this is discovered it is pulled down and fixed, repaired, or altered to match the event. The school nurse reported that Nancy Lanza was a nice kindergartner teacher, only to find out Nancy Lanza was never a school teacher there. There is the tribute video that was posted a month before the event on *VIMEO* web page. This video points out on the web page that viewers had traveled to that page back in November, way ahead of the shooting.

Let's look at Ryan Lanza and his identity confusion. Adam Lanza is found with his brothers identification card in the school. His brother Ryan is arrested and charged with the shooting before they find out it was not Ryan, but Adam. They report no one had seen Adam for three years and his brother hadn't seen him for two years. So how is it he has his brothers identification card?

There is FEMA L-366 planning for the needs of children in disasters, dated December 14, 2012 which is located on the Department of Emergency service & Public service, Emergency and management Homeland Security page, under what appears to be a scheduled calendar event. Interesting how this page was created so quickly, though if it were scheduled would make sense.

Emilie Parker was pictured with the President after the shooting. How could she be seen with the President after the shooting if she were one of the victims? Though this could explain why Robbie Parker was seen earlier smiling.

The SSDI (Social Security Death Index) states Adam Lanza died on December 12, 2012, two days before the shooting occurred. He killed twenty six and wounded one, making him very accurate with the death to injury ratio, being 26 to 1.

Apparently Connecticut has an assault rifle ban making it a class D felony. Where and how did Nancy Lanza acquire this weapon and how was Adam so skilled at using this weapon? Lt. Vance stated they had investigators looking at who every weapon belong to.

If Adam Lanza worked alone who was the guy that people saw in the woods handcuffed? A gentleman being interviewed stated a man walked by them saying he didn't do it. The gentleman being interviewed at the time stated, "he is in the back of the police car now. He was dressed in cameo pants and a dark jacket." Who was this guy and where is he now? According to the video you hear an officer say there are two shooters seen running. One was supposedly an off duty police officer from out of town, who just happened to get caught in the woods with only one road that lead in to the school? Was he the second shooter, or was he the one in the police vehicle?

Dawn Hochsprung had implemented a new security system prior to the shooting. Where is that video evidence at?

During all the videos you see not one victim being assisted by EMS, Law Enforcement. There is no blood, there is no video showing the children escaping.

What we do see is a staging area, one at the school and one at the church. We see no first responders moving in any manner as to help with victims, but rather just standing around as though they too are waiting for something to occur, rather than something that had occurred. We do not see bodies being brought out and loaded in ambulances. We see people walking around what at first looks just like confusion, but if you watch the many characters out there you will see they are walking routes that make this all appear to be more organized or scripted.

If you look at the 911 transcripts you will see the first caller called in at 9:35 am while another lady called in at 9:56 am. She was asking for ambulances and states she is outside and there appears to be none out there. Why would it take twenty minutes to get ambulances there? The dispatcher confirmed that they had been called because he stated yea they're coming. Then at the end of that he stated "We will have them come right now, ok." Why would you have to say that if they were already coming?

The second call came in approximately 17 seconds later by a caller who is distressed asking also for an ambulance. Third caller contacts 911 dispatch who answers, "Are you calling about the shooting in Newtown?" The caller states yes he is calling in about the shooting and states he is not injured. He states he is calling from the other school?

He states he was not involved, but that he just arrived and needs an ambulances on scene.

A caller told 911 dispatch to bring ambulance at base of school they're bringing victims out there. The ambulances never make it to the base of the school for some reason. A caller states we need assistance in the kindergartner room #3. This call was at approximately 10 am. Finally Ambulances arrive, but they still need more ambulances. They talk about how there are three injured yet at the time Adam Lanza was supposedly found dead as he took his own life. They do not mention anything about deceased personnel Which they would have had to see if they went by room 8 and room 10 according to the reporter. On another call they stated that they would need multiple ambulances and they had multiple KIA (killed in action).

When we look at United Way, we see they created a page to collect funds to help with the Sandy Hook travesty. The problem is they too jumped the gun and published their page well in advance of the Sandy Hook shooting. On the Google page there was a link that said (Sandy Hook School Support Fund) The document date page showed December 11,2012, Days before the shooting

The United Way of Western Connecticut said it rejects conspiracies theories, claiming it knew about December 14th Newtown Connecticut school shooting three days in advance and leveraged that knowledge to raise money. The New Way fund was actually established by the Newtown savings bank. The president and CEO of the bank is none other than John Trentacosta. The very same Trentacosta that owned the home next to the Lanzas.

There is aerial photos that show both the Lanza and the Trentacosta residences, which show tire tracks only in the driveway and grass of the Trentacosta property. The Lanza property, which was the area considered to be the area of interest due to Adam Lanza being the identified shooter, had no sign of activity to very little activity. There is also photos showing there was a road block at the end of the Trentacosta driveway. Why were they blocking that driveway and not the Lanza's driveway?

According to the reporters, John Trentacosta stated the fund was created due to countless requests. If we look at this as true, then when did he receive these requests? The reason I mention this is because this page was up and running at minimum on the same day of the shooting. That means someone developed the fund concept. You would have needed a planning meeting. You would also need to establish a fund account and coordinate with the United Way foundation. You would need to develop a campaign. You would need to create the art work web context and layout. Then publish this all on line.

This by itself makes it look as though there was knowledge of the incident going to take place ahead of when it did. You could almost call it a version of insider trading, whether it was for the purpose of gaining money, power, or political favors is hard to say, but not out of the realm.

If we look at the DNA evidence, we see more doubt and questions that once again don't add up.

There is the 22 Savage rifle, a Christmas card, an envelope, labeled for the students of Sandy Hook elementary school, the adhesive side of the stamp, and the exterior and interior of the door handles of the car located at the crime scene. They then got a DNA sample from Nancy Lanza's blood and from the person said to be the alleged Adam Lanza, getting a sample from his liver, so as to compare the DNA.

Based on the conclusion by the Forensic Science Examiner, Nancy was eliminated as a contributor and was eliminated from all items. Adam was eliminated as a contributor from the following items as well, however the only items that were swabbed that he could be connected to would be mixers. A DNA mixer is a sample that contains more than one individual's DNA.

You may ask how can more than one persons DNA be present if Adam Lanza acted alone? Was the DNA contaminated? On January 17, 2013 a hit was made to a convicted offender's DNA profile from the New York State Police Investigation Center. Who was this guy and how was he connected to the school or the Lanzas?

Eric Hurita the Forensic Examiner received an email asking questions of concern on the following questions. Would your conclusions indicate any of the following?

#1 Adam Lanza was not the shooter?

#2 Adam Lanza did not work alone?

#3 There was somebody else definitely involved?

#4 Was there any follow up on the convict from New York and if your findings put him as one of your suspects?

#5 Do you know the context of what was found inside the letter and why it was crucial to the investigation?

#6 The DNA swab that was taken from Adam Lanza was taken from his liver, is this common procedure?

#7 Were you ever brought into contact with the shooters body or was the liver swab the only source of Adam Lanzas DNA? According to the report he has yet to reply to the questions that we Americans want and deserve. Is the reason he can't answer because it is still ongoing, or is he afraid of self incrimination?

Let us look at Barbara Sibley, who during her interview stated her son had forgot something and when she arrived she could tell something wasn't right. She states there were eight or ten kids running towards the fire house. Who were these eight or ten kids? You will see Barbara arrives before the police, while a subject is still shooting. Were these kids running to the fire house or were these the ones that went to Gene Rosen's house?

She mentioned seeing a black hatchback and it was by the entrance and all the doors were open and jackets laying on the ground outside the doors of the vehicle. She saw another mom by the door and they mentioned how quiet it sounded then they noticed the broken glass and heard shots being fired.

She talks about seeing the kids leave as they are being escorted and she describes the event as organized as the children are being led by their teachers They show a picture with a girl running with her and in the interview she mentions her son. She states she sees her son but doesn't want him to see her hysterical? Really I would not care about anything but holding my child and blessing God for keeping him safe.

In the photo you see two women running with a girl and an officer, while another officer is seen in the background looking away from the building and what appears to be a third officer outside the door as well. Should not those three officers attack and eliminate the threat, rather than assist people that are temporarily safe in the parking lot?

The subjects vehicle is found to belong to a Christopher Rodia. So did Christopher report his car stolen, or was he one of the shooters as well?

One of the kids stated he heard a loud bang and thought something fell, then he heard another and thought it was gunshots. The teacher Katelyn Roy stated it happened during their meeting. When asked what happened she stated, the shooting. The first class room, she states and that she knew it was gunshots because it came from one of those guns that shoots over and over again. She stated she shut her door but didn't lock it? She stated she had them all get in the bathroom all 15 students plus herself. She stacked them in the small bathroom One of the boys stated he knew karate. She told him he needed to just remain where they were and remain calm.

One of the other kids stated during this ordeal that their teacher was reading them books and keeping them calm. Maybe this kid had a different teacher. The reporter on the video also mentioned there were candles that the children drew but when you looked at the candles they seemed to be taped on the windows so as to view them from outside, rather than from inside like you would expect. There are also shelves and file cabinets that are placed in front of them in the classroom. It appears odd to me and again appears staged for those that would be reporting to see this easily from outside, rather than from inside.

President Obama talked on his frustration with two and a half years left, stating "That this society has not been willing to take some basic steps to keep guns out of the hands of people who can do unbelievable damage. We are the only developed country on earth where this happens. It now happens once a week. It's a one day story, there is no place else like this." He talks about 26 year olds getting gunned down and this town couldn't do anything about it. Maybe he meant 26 people, referring to Sandy Hook, Connecticut.

This is why many people feel there is a hidden agenda and a secret that has been silenced from the rest of the public. The question then becomes, did anyone truly die? Was it a drill, or a drill gone bad? Were some people in on it, or was the whole town of Sandy Hook aware of this so called travesty?

The world deserves answers and answers come from questions that are asked or evidence that is uncovered, or revealed.

It appears the whole world is a stage

Are these the children that were savagely killed, or are they pictures of children that are now adult actors or accomplices with a cause?

Top picture An officer at an active shooting with his gun still in his holster and another officer with his back toward the school where the threat is supposedly coming from?

This is a statement by a Newtown resident. I thought it sounded very interesting.

"I live in Newtown CT. I will post no proof that I actually do live here. I am sure some have clicked away immediately at that confession and I do not blame them. You may or may not believe in what I am about to say and that is your choice.

I live in Newtown, I live about a mile from Sandy Hook Elementary on Riverside Road. I didn't go to work on December 14th, I called in sick, but I was playing hooky. I work at a restaurant in Danbury. I've spent the past two hours debating with myself if I should post this.

I could have posted this somewhere else, but this site seems to always pop up when the Sandy Hook shooting is concerned. I figured this was the most popular spot.

At around 8:50- 9:00am I had just finished eating my breakfast. I had Captain Crunch cereal. I had used the last of the milk. I decided to go get some at Caraluzzi's, because a friend of mine works there and I wanted to see what he was up to that evening. I get in my car at about 9:05am. I drive West on Riverside Road.

Before I even got to the fire house, I notice a lot of vehicles parked there. Way, way, way more than usual. A few were parked on both sides of the road. I figured they were just doing some kind of training or meeting.

However one thing did stick out and that was the fact that a lot of the vehicles were solid silver and solid black. I drove past the Fire House and the senior center is right next door less than a hundred yards. That parking lot was full as well, with some of the same vehicles mixed with trucks and what not. Vehicles you would expect to see in a parking lot. Still I thought nothing of it. I go get my milk.

I'm in Carraluzzi's and I've been talking to my friend for a right good while and we hear two police vehicles go by. About five minutes later we hear a Helicopter. Dave comes from the back and said, "They must be doing another drill again. Scanner said mass casualty incident involving children." Right then I figured out why all those vehicles were at the Fire House and Senior Center, because it is not the first time they have done that. They did a similar thing about a year ago, around this time of year and they are always doing car accidents that concern Hazmat, or whatever. I told them what I saw. Dave said, "Those cars sound like FBI cars. I guess they would be in on it.

So I figured I'd go, so I could catch a peek at what was going on. I get to town and couldn't go down Riverside Road. I told the officer that I live down there. He said, "No through traffic even for residents. Fire and Rescue and Police need to finish what they are doing."

I said, "What are they doing?" He said, "I would tell you if I knew and I have no clue.

The way it sounds they are running a drill, but we have been blocked from main traffic. I was just told to do traffic control and make sure no one goes down there."

Then I drive West to Danbury. I don't know why I just did. I was thinking to myself that is what I get for playing hooky from work. I had the radio on, but not loud enough to hear. I turn it up thinking maybe I could catch what is going on.

The local station mentioned nothing. At about 10:00am they break in from Sammy Hagar's "I can't drive 55". The guy said he was hearing reports of an incident at Sandy Hook Elementary and that surrounding schools were on lockdown , however "I called my wife because she works at Newtown Middle School and she said they weren't on lockdown and hadn't heard anything about an incident. So it appears information has been mixed up. We need to get our stuff together before they tell me to report".

I get to Danbury and I go into Global gas station to get a Mt. Dew. They had the TV on and I froze. They were watching coverage of the shooting. I just watched for thirty minutes frozen. Then I started thinking about all those cars at the Fire Department. I didn't know what to think about that. My brain just didn't work after watching the television.

Fast forward to right this second. I've read the theories and the stories and honestly, those are the only ones that add up. I live here and I do not know what the **** went on. This town is fairly small. I know right many people. I know Eugene Rosen. He is an extremely creepy bastard. I know Scarlett Lewis. But I would like to know where in the hell she got all that money to spruce herself up for interviews.

But the phelps and Parker families that seemed to be shoved down our throats, I have no idea in hell who they are. I've asked families and friends and they don't know who they are. I know a Robert Parker, but that sure as hell isn't him in the interviews. I just do not know what is going on.

The narrator says, what you are about to see are pages from a DHS (Department of Homeland Security)school shooting exercise plan, for a drill in Iowa that happened back in 2011. Looking at the context you see it states you need to arrive at your appropriate site fifteen minutes early. Wear the appropriate uniform and identification items. Sign in when you arrive.

Parking information and directions to each venue area are available from the Emergency Management Agency. Refreshments and portable water will be provided for all exercise participants throughout the exercise. Restroom facilities will be available at each venue.

Identification badges will be issued to the exercise staff. All exercise personnel and observers will be identified by agency uniforms and, or identification badges distributed by the exercise staff. They show a chart that describes these identification items. The badge colors represent the type of group as follows.

White: Exercise Director

Black: Exercise staff

Green: Controllers

Red: Evaluators

Orange: Actors

Yellow: Support Staff

Blue: Observers

Pink: Media Personnel

None: Players uninformed

Gray: Players in civilian Clothes

They showed pictures of stacks of bottled water set up inside one of the buildings in Newtown, Ct. The similarities are hard not to see. People gathered around and appear not as worried and confused, some personnel, possibly actors who are waiting to play their roles. We must remember shadows may depict more than one thing, creating an illusion of alternatives.

Let's look at Noah Pozner. A video on you tube shows him as a victim of a school shooting, not just of Sandy Hook Elementary, but as a victim of a school shooting in Pakistan. A British Boxer known as Amir Kahn visited a school in Pakistan where the Taliban massacred a hundred and fifty two people December 30,2014. He wanted to help scarred children return to school. I wonder if after being killed twice in two different countries, in two different school shootings Noah Pozner will be better prepared when the third school shooting takes place?

A picture is worth a thousand words, but a video speaks volumes. Noah's mother talked of her son and showed no sign of sadness. She tried to express herself as being numb to the News Media, as she portrays herself as deprived of the power of sensation. The problem is that Noah's mom wants us to share in her grieving process, while she has yet to show any signs of grieving. She is in front of the media on her own and was not forced to talk to the world, yet only speaks of her son, not about him. She too brings up guns rather than dealing with the shooters mental capacity.

She focuses on the AR assault rifle, describing it as though it were the cause of a tormented soul. When asked what her objective was with this, she stated "I haven't wrapped my head around it yet, I'm certainly no Statesman women." We will get back to that statement.

When Veronique Pozner talked on another interview she mentioned her son was a twin, but failed to mention that on the other interview. She was asked if she were afraid the death of her child might be all for nothing. She stated, "If we haven't reached critical mass. If there isn't some type of change in the national consciousness, by six and seven year olds being gun down in the sanctity of their own school then I think we have lost true North in this country. Our compass is broken and our priorities are completely off kilter." Even the interviewer was amazed at how she could talk about this without losing composer.

She states she's not always composed, that she cries every day, but she is just a private person. You could say in front of the camera she is always composed. If you remember Veronique stated , I'm certainly no Statesman women. You will see in one of the video links she Veronique Haller Pozner is a legal counselor for the Government of Switzerland. You can reach her directly in the Switzerland Embassy in Washington, DC.

Myself watching from the outside, have to ask are these things all anomalies? I am a Correctional officer I am trained in observation, what doesn't make sense today may mean everything tomorrow. Let me give a simple example using a picture of Emily with President Obama.

If the picture was taken after the shooting then how is she not reported as a survivor rather than a victim?

If the picture was taken before the shooting, you then have to ask why was the President there in the first place and again have to ask, what are the odds a child that gets to meet the President of the United States is then massacred.

Remember I stated we had to look at everyone as suspects, looking at Nancy Lanza's neighbors all of them seem to know nothing of her or of Adam. It is as though they were placed in a setting and went into hiding. No one seems to have ever been inside their home, no one?

Adam Lanza seemed to have disappeared in 2009 after his sophomore year. He is seen as being autistic yet is able to go to college having not gone through his junior and senior years in high school? He is able to wipe his computer so clean leaving nothing for the trained FBI investigators to find for evidence? He was able to kill 26 people leaving only one casualty, or three at the most? Maybe Adam Lanza is the real Glimmer Man. One girl named Israel who claims she is a classmate of Adams then states she never was actually in any of his classes? States she never seen him with anyone and that he would always sit alone at lunch. She mentioned Nancy Lanza as a kindergartner teacher when she wasn't.

The investigators mention that during the shooting spree that approximately 150 rounds were shot. Where are all the bullet holes, not including the ricochets which each shot can produce multiple shot markings.

Where is the video of Adam Lanza entering the
school? They supposedly put up cameras and people had
to be identified to get in to the school. It is interesting
that the cameras we want to view we can't, while the
other cameras are all over the place as everyone is
strolling and patrolling to be seen and heard.

There is more videos out there in regards to this
travesty. There are more questions that still need answers.
During the one interview where Gene Rosen is talking
you see a sign in the back flashing. The sign says,
(Everyone must check in.) If we remember just a little
while ago I had talked about that Iowa drill, where that
was part of the protocol. You had to sign in when you
arrived. When you watch videos of the Sandy Hook
shooting you see people with ID's on. Find out more on
those Id's and you might be amazed.

Charlotte Bacon, 2/22/06, female
- **Daniel Barden**, 9/25/05, male
- **Rachel Davino**, 7/17/83, female.
- **Olivia Engel**, 7/18/06, female
- **Josephine Gay**, 12/11/05, female
- **Ana M. Marquez-Greene**, 04/04/06, female
- **Dylan Hockley**, 3/8/06, male
- **Dawn Hochsprung**, 06/28/65, female
- **Madeleine F. Hsu**, 7/10/06, female
- **Catherine V. Hubbard**, 6/08/06, female
- **Chase Kowalski**, 10/31/05, male
- **Jesse Lewis**, 6/30/06, male
- **James Mattioli** , 3/22/06, male
- **Grace McDonnell**, 12/04/05, female
- **Anne Marie Murphy**, 07/25/60, female
- **Emilie Parker**, 5/12/06, female
- **Jack Pinto**, 5/06/06, male
- **Noah Pozner**, 11/20/06, male
- **Caroline Previdi**, 9/07/06, female
- **Jessica Rekos**, 5/10/06, female
- **Avielle Richman**, 10/17/06, female
- **Lauren Rousseau**, 6/1982, female (full date of birth not specified)
- **Mary Sherlach**, 2/11/56, female
- **Victoria Soto**, 11/04/85, female
- **Benjamin Wheeler**, 9/12/06, male
- **Allison N. Wyatt**, 7/03/06, female

Highlighted names appear in photo to the left from a photo taken February 2013 supposedly.

If these are the kids that were said to be killed we should be happy knowing they are all alive, however this is not the case, Americans are mad if this is what happened. We are tired of being lied to and deceived through deception. It is important to know we can trust our government, to know they will tell us the truth, the whole truth so help them God.

What is interesting is that the Sandy Hook School was tore down and destroyed. The home of Nancy and Adam Lanza was tore down and destroyed. The Virginia Tech School is still up and running after the shooting that took place on April 16,2007, killing 32 and wounding 17 others in two separate attacks. The Columbine School is still up and running after the April 20, 1999 shooting, killing 13 people. The McDonald massacre that took place in 1984, where forty bystanders were shot twenty one died, it too continued to operate.

When I compared some of the videos that are on You Tube you saw law enforcement moving with a purpose. You see students outside running, confused in chaos. Nothing on those other events show any signs of masking. Was the house and school destroyed to rid them of any evidence that might be left? Look at who was Commander in Chief at the time of these events? President Reagan 1984 McDonald Massacre, President Clinton 1999Columbine shooting, President George W. Bush 2007 Virginia Tech Massacre, President Obama 2012 Sandy Hook.

Francine Lopez Wheeler was identified as one of the parents of Benjamin Wheeler, who died during a mass shooting at Sandy Hook Elementary. She is a former personal assistant to the Finance Chair Woman and the Democratic Committee, Maureen White. Both Maureen and her husband Steven Rattner are members of the Council of Foreign Relations. Steven Rattner is known to have ruffled feathers with gun control advocate Michael Bloomberg according to the New York Times. Francine is an actor and singer. She became the first person other than Obama and Biden to deliver the White House weekly address. She identified herself as just a citizen.

Mark Barden, parent of alleged victim Daniel Barden is a lifelong entertainer, composer and musician, is shown on the White House. Gov. website. Barden leads policy on outreach efforts for sandy Hook promise, an organization that is committed to affecting policy in mental health, gun access, and enhanced security.

Nicole Hockley, mother of Dylan Hockley graduated from Trinity College, where she majored in English and theater. She publicly admitted regret of not continuing her acting career.

Jimmy Green father of Anna Marquez, is an entertainer and musician, both Jim and his wife are strong advocates for gun control. It appears that many of the children come from families who were in to the entertainment society, and or political parties with certain agendas such as gun control.

The truth is hard to find when you talk about Sandy Hook. Because it is the inconsistencies that make us want to take another look at this travesty. If this were a movie people would be asking for their money back as the script would be seen as poorly written. There are too many holes that leave doubt and suspicion.

The characters too appear to be lost in how they portray themselves. No one is seen with tears when they should. Their behaviors too appear fake and insincere. The timing is off in many areas that we had discussed. The children evacuating the school is not caught on tape or seen in photos other than two photos that appear to be staged using a couple of the same children.

The School is destroyed along with Nancy Lanza's home leaving again less evidence as to make it appear suspicious, getting rid of evidence that could later be looked at. I am not saying anyone is guilty or innocent, I am leaving that to you to decide. There is a lot more out there that could be looked at and if you are interested I have included some links that you can check out yourself and see what I saw.

The following are links to sites on YouTube that will get you thinking.

https://www.youtube.com/watch?v=X3aYQEJXJfo

https://www.youtube.com/watch?v=aQz1BIM9mLw

https://www.youtube.com/watch?v=oD0z275nQnM

https://www.youtube.com/watch?v=lV20DtXBuQs

https://www.youtube.com/watch?v=Hvhs5PWQW-o

https://www.youtube.com/watch?v=iCGDFUWVyG8

https://www.youtube.com/watch?v=3uZqtWWqD0E

https://www.youtube.com/watch?v=eYwPN5-FDoc

https://www.youtube.com/watch?v=ivt1KzZ9Bs8

https://www.youtube.com/watch?v=WmJO3ljBy7Y

https://www.youtube.com/watch?v=AUSJ6rqEWUY

Compare these videos to the videos of the other mass shootings and you will see the obvious. Let the truth speak for itself. If you are ready we will move on to our next story, as Deception, shadows of truth continues.

JADE HELM

The world as we know it is changing. We have a president that bows to our allies, he refuses to confront Muslim Extremists. He opens his arms as he closes his eyes telling those that wish to kill us he trusts them, while making nuclear deals with our enemies.

Recently a military exercise took place in multiple states from July 15,2015 through September 15,2015. It involved unconventional warfare, using the United States Army Special Operations Command and Joint Special Operations Command, along with other U.S. military forces. It involved the States of Texas, Arizona, Florida, Louisiana, Mississippi, New Mexico, and Utah.

The troops were categorized as occupying or resistant forces. They operated near small towns and some wore civilian clothes and drove civilian vehicles. It was said to involve approximately 1200 troops.

According to CNN mainly Army Green Beret and a small amount of Navy Seals, along with Air Force Special Operations Troops, also including regular Army infantry there as well.

Lt. Col. Mark Lastoria, at an information session for residents in Bastrop, Texas, said the realistic military training helps soldiers adapt to unfamiliar terrain. In that location, sixty soldiers would take part, including the presence of two Humvee vehicles and a "water buffalo" water tank. Private land offered by residents would be used for the exercise. He noted they would not be paid for the land or receive a tax break of any kind. Lastoria also claimed $150,000 in revenue would be brought to the area because of food, fuel, and shopping.

Were the owners of the private property willing participants or did they not have a choice? It sounded like Lt. Col. Mark Lastoria wanted to make it look good by stating it would bring more money to the area of Bastrop. The problem is that many people see this as nothing more than subterfuge. Let's look at a few key factors. The first one is how long is this exercise for? If it is just a short term than why do they mention not compensating the property owners. Why would that be an issue? How does it bring in more money when it is a military operation that is just a short term exercise, or is it?

Many believe that it is the start of a more secret sinister plan, known as Martial Law. Many think they are incorporating military exercises in civilian areas to get people comfortable with seeing them all over, while they secretly move in more and more military personnel and equipment.

The Austin American Statesman newspaper noted that after plans and maps of the exercise were made public the social media exploded. The map showed areas that were considered hostile, including Texas and Utah.

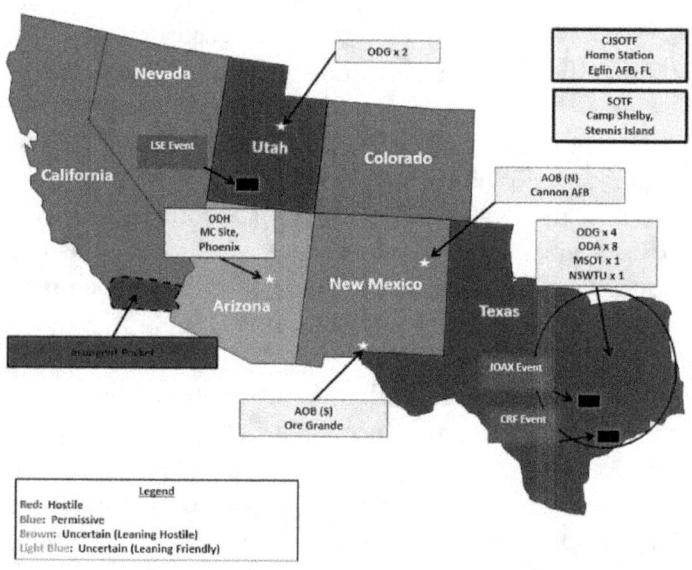

Lt. Col. Mark Lastoria also commented stating it was to get the soldiers accustomed to unfamiliar terrain? Show me any area of terrain we have not already experienced, in training at our military sites or in actual combat throughout the history of our existence? The only other terrain would be civilian terrain, putting our homes and property on the battlefield.

On May 2,2015 Republican presidential candidate and Texas Senator Ted Cruz reached out to the Pentagon to inquire about the exercise.

At the South Carolina Republican Party's annual convention Senator Cruz said, "We are assured it is a military training exercise. I have no reason to doubt those assurances, but I understand the reason for concern and uncertainty, because when the federal government has not demonstrated itself to be trustworthy in this administration, the natural consequence is that many citizens don't trust what it is saying".

U.S. Representative Louie Gohmert, from the 1st District of Texas, on May 5,2015 stated his office has been overwhelmed with calls referring to the Jade Helm 15 military exercises. The concerns that the U.S. Army is preparing for modern day martial law. He stated he was appalled that the hostile areas, have a republican majority, cling to their guns and religion. He stated the map for the exercise needs to change names on the map and the tone needs to be revamped so the federal government is not intentionally practicing war against its own States.

Jessie Ventura, Former Navy Seal, feels it is to get us use to a military presence, where we except it. Like myself, Jessie Ventura believes their excuse for getting accustomed to unfamiliar terrain is nothing more than a ruse. They have terrain available in all the military bases they have specialized training in mountain warfare, urban warfare, desert training, cold weather training, and much more. This goes back a couple of years ago according to Jessie Ventura, when the Defense Department and John McCain put in an amendment giving the U.S. military the ability to be allowed total access to anywhere inside the U.S. borders.

Under the Jade Helm conspiracy theories, Government will establish martial law. Government will be responsible for shutting down the Blue Bell Creameries. The idea government is responsible for the excessive rain in Texas, along with the shutdown of the Wal-Mart stores then turned into prisons for personnel to be locked up securely.

On You Tube there is a video showing two semis belonging to Wal-Mart that are in the midst of a military convoy. When you look at the other map it shows flags all over, maybe these are the Wal-Mart stores that are located throughout our country. If you think about it if the government took over using martial law, all the Wal-Mart's are not only scattered everywhere throughout the U.S. but they are of the same design making it easy to convert them all the same way using one blue print.

On one of the video links I have included, you will see President Bush showing his appreciation to Sam Walton and his wife Helen, the owner of Wal-Mart as he talks about showing his respect to a man who through his hard work, vision, and treating people right, many good things can happen. They talk about Wal-Mart making our communities more safe and secure. A woman on television states, "If you see something suspicious in the parking lot, or in the store say something immediately. The Wal-Mart stores are completely covered inside and out with cameras making it hard to hide. A news reporter talks to one of the vehicle operators of an MRAP (Mine Resistant Ambush Protected) vehicle. The reporter stated it seems appropriate to use this type vehicle in Iraq, but why here, as she interviews him outside of Wal-Mart?

The operator said, "we have a lot of constitutionalists who are stock piling a lot of weapons and a lot of ammunition. The last I knew it was our constitutional right. Who is this person to question the constitution? He is wearing a uniform but the patch appears to be unidentifiable. They also show the American flag with the Chinese flag joined together on one pin.

On the video they state, the communist Chinese storm troopers are working directly with the United States Military industrial complex, which has been hijacked by the council on foreign relations, Bilderberg Group, Trilateral Commission, and subsequently the United Nations. The Chinese have publicly stated to disarm the citizens.

Xinhau is the official Chinese news agency. It has demanded that the U.S. immediately adopt stricter gun control measures to reduce the number of firearms the populist are permitted to possess. If this is a joint effort to take away our guns then every American is at risk. They say that the Wal-Mart's are going to be detention centers. If we look at one more thing we could say they are currently stores that ware house lots of goods from food, clothing, hardware, guns and more. Wal-Mart's are national now in many, many countries. If the military incorporates itself like Wal-Mart did we will not think anything about it till it is too late.

Make sure when you observe our soldiers out there you look at their patches are they still flying the American flag or is our flag vanishing and another flag appearing?

The D.O.D.(Department of Defense) admits it has become treasonously Rogue. In the same video it mentions the Litmus test and asks if you would be willing to kill Americans? I think that is a red flag that ought to be addressed. Maybe the red flag is just China? Some law enforcement personnel were asked if they would work with federal agencies, to try and take guns from American citizens. They even asked Chris Kyle the Famous American sniper and head of Craft International, if they could use his civilian contracting slash Para military forces to steal peoples guns. That is supposedly from his direct testimony. They refer to that is why he was killed, because he wasn't playing ball and he was talking to too many people.

They mention the UNODA (United Nations Office for Disarmament affairs) they also mention The Asian Pacific Union of the Trilateral Commission that is the number one contributor to the United Nations. We now have the Communist foot soldiers here on our soil.

Why do our American soldiers hold the Chinese flag outside the White House, along with ours? It is just another red flag we should pay attention too. Hillary Clinton was discussed on this video selling out our military to the communist through her hidden emails

The CFR (Council on Foreign Relations stated Terrorist proxy Armies are it's only option now. This organization was founded in 1921. It is a United States nonprofit, 4,900 member organization, publisher, and think tank specializing in U.S. foreign policy and international affairs. They mention the movie Red Dawn, it speaks for itself, just watch the movie.

The President of the United States, President Obama has gone executive order excessive, it appears our check and balance system is not checking, or balancing. Many theorists feel Obama is going to create a scenario to justify his martial Law agenda. I hope we are all wrong about this.

We could ask why did we go all of a sudden through such a stringent time, where ammunition became scarce and hard to get? Why do they have limits on how much you can buy? Why did Wal-Mart band certain caliber guns, if even for just a short time? Everything points to elimination of guns and the Americans constitutional rights.

Why does the Homeland security warn against Right Wing Radicals, when its leader can't say the word Muslim extremist? Christianity is constantly being attacked, as they try taking the word God out of our society, one House at a time. Freedom of religion, gun owners right to bear arms, all these are motives for them to create a military capable of forcing us to follow their agenda and guidelines. I hope I am wrong but many people see this as what is happening.

The Bible has been under attack it's been banned from many federal buildings and State Capitals. The Christmas tree, now called the Holiday tree, really what holiday are they celebrating? President Obama has crucified the actions of the Christians while showing passive submissive behavior toward the Muslim Extremists. When you look at all this, it makes you think it will not just be another Civil War, but a Holy War. The only thing I know about that, is those that stand with God will win.

The Department of Defense has released a new list of those we need to watch on that list, ahead of the Muslims and Mosque, are the Evangelical Christians. There is a newly released military manual that has been leaked. They mention the killing of Americans in civil disturbance operations. Those that rise up against them.

Reported over the televised networks, a military exercise along the Chicago river showing three Black Hawk helicopters in a tight formation. A military drill in downtown Miami with Black Hawk helicopters. Other news reporting a joint military and police task force operation as they report hearing gunshots and police with lights and sirens. Armed men in fatigues with plenty of weapons in Houston patrolling the area. There was Ottawa, Illinois April 25, 2013 six helicopters hovering overhead as spectators watched in awe. They report military exercises involving helicopters hovering over banks in Los Angeles. The entire city of Boston is on lockdown in the suburb of Watertown. They were searching door to door as the town was swarmed with law enforcement, federal agents, and military personnel.

They talk about a one world government currency. China wants one world currency. France wants a new world order, and Obama seems to be directing us into the same path. They talk about gold and oil being higher and currency becoming weaker.

On Bill O'Reilly's show the O'Reilly Factor they say, "If the feds do not stop the wild spending, the U.S. dollar will collapse. That means that all of your savings, investments, your home and everything else will blow up before your eyes."

There is talk of the RFID Microchip being implemented. You ask what is the purpose for this? They want to introduce it as a tool that can assist doctors. You have this chip embedded inside you for quick access to the doctor, so he will have all your medical records available to him.

There is on one video where the military is processing civilians and you hear them say over the loud speaker "Attention, attention, attention American forces are here to help. We will not tolerate civil disobedience." They talk about Jade Helm being a nationwide military exercise, which makes some sense, due to the uniforms appearing to be different. From patches and the uniform itself. The troops will operate under cover in local populations.

Rick Perry the former Governor of Texas, states it is ok to question your government but you should not question the military. I think he must have forgotten that the military falls under the executive branch of our government. Of course he may have been preoccupied with running as a presidential candidate. You would think he would know the different branches of government. It might just be politicians don't always think before they speak. Getting back to the RFID microchip.

If you can implement that chip how about a chip that has all your records, from bank accounts, to political party allies, along with the ability to track you where ever you go so they know everything about you. Their goal is to get rid of money and you just purchase items through a chip. If you challenge them your chip gets turned off and you can't purchase anything. This sounds bizarre but let me introduce you to another part of Jade Helm.

Jade II

As you know Jade Helm is about the military operating in secret along side of us in the civilian world. But there is however another part of Jade Helm even more secret an intrusive, behind Jade Helm is Jade II. It is an AI software system using quantum computing. Quantum computers are different from digital electronic computers based on transistors.

It has the ability to collect immeasurable amounts of data on humans to generate a humane terrain system they talk about this in their PDF. In geographical location used to identify, eliminate targets, insurgents, rebels, or any labels that can be flagged as targets on a global information grid.

John W. Whitehead, the Founder of the Rutherford Institute has a book out called Battlefield America. He brings out the worst scenarios for mankind. A book well worth reading.

On the YouTube video they talk about artificial intelligence and algorithms. They mention behind the scenes where much is hidden in secrecy. The software they developed is Jade II. They mention its technology will not be battles directed by Generals and Commanders, but by a computer. The lady talks about the documents that lay out what this computer system can do and will do.

This system uses vast sums of information collected on individuals, groups, populations, regions, large geographical areas and, or countries.

It inputs all that information in to a module called HTA (Human Terrain Analyst) tool, which than analyzes the data then develops an HTS (Humane Terrain System). Once it is established it determines behavioral parameters for norms of individuals, groups, populations, geographic areas etc.

The establishment of these parameters is known as the human domain. It can then identify, extract, or eliminate perceived threats or targets based on deviations from these norms. Jade II can also examine the humane terrain system over time with the use of thousands of remote sensors, both audio and visual, along with real time communication and monitoring. It can write or rewrite its own parameters on particular human domain.

The information can be retrieved at anytime for any reason. It can create battle plans in seconds vs. hours or weeks. It can create battlefield simulations on the fly. A CBR (Case base regional) module receives a mission statement to produce an adaptive course of action. It adapts to the ever changing human domain. It adapts its plans on us, based on humane terrain based on human activity.

Your human activity would be your communications, bank account transactions, travel patterns, habits, behavior patterns, your emotions. The system can read human emotion. It can write its own COA (Course of Action) on the fly.

Does this sound impossible? Does it sound terrifying, as we then become helpless slaves of our own making.

This system is aware, it is aware of the ever changing. They state there is no central input data point. The huge data dump centers are connected to this global information grid. It is the NSA that is collecting data on everyone not just those labeled as threats. The reason that they are collecting data, the woman on the video states, is the government perceives Americans as its greatest threat. She states they will use a computer based military to clamp us down. Patriots will be classified as terrorists, the true terrorists which is the government out there will receive its directives and agendas from the ruling elite. They will be seen as patriots to be protected at all costs.

Jade II can predict conflict before it occurs and react in a preemptive measure. It thinks in the present, but can predict future events, or human activity. It can make decisions regarding casualties and targets in regards to the overall objective of the mission. The system holds itself accountable for its own actions It holds total command and control of all information over land, sea, air, space, and cyberspace, that is how it will master the human terrain. This is said in the PDF and the software.

The Jade II has no moral compass, sympathy, or regrets. It will be Man vs. Machine. The futuristic world we watch on television for entertainment purposes will now be us in reality. Yes this is scary and hard to accept, but check out these videos yourself and tell me there is not something going on.

Let us continue on now that you have a brief overview of Jade II.

When we look at one of the Wal-Mart stores in Tulsa, Oklahoma that was said to had closed for plumbing issues, we see two officers who mention it is actually getting gutted. There is talk that Wal-Mart was closing underperforming stores. Employees state it is because of labor disputes.

On GMN network they mention about Facebook and Wal-Mart helping to write rules on facial recognition technology. Stating they are connecting with the Department of Homeland Security with their data base. They state if you do not want to be recognized then do not go into a Wal-Mart store. They also mentioned during Hurricane Katrina that Wal-Mart in Bentonville, Arkansas was working with DHS to create an emergency operation center and coordinating with Homeland Security for the purpose of supply distribution.

On one of the videos you will see a military convoy at Union Station, which is out of Portland, Oregon. On that video you will see these big crates and when they show you the inside of them you see where guns will be stored these are for the purpose of collecting guns and no other reason.

They talk about the tunnels under some of the Wal-Mart stores and on some links show pictures of these huge tunnels. They show where they have added concertina wire, or razor wire to the top of one of these closed Wal-Mart stores it shows it going around the whole building. This wire has only two purposes that I can think of, and that is to keep people out, or in.

They also mention on SHTF Plan.com about an article where it says, **Revealed: Government to resurrect old Wal-Mart as prison. Railroad terminus sits directly adjacent.** In Flathead county of Montana, an unincorporated town adjacent to Kalispell. The primary reason listed for the purchase of the facility was for an expansion of the county jail. They state Wal-Mart is 130,000 square feet. The current jail is built to house 63 prisoners, convicts, detainees, or civilians. So when you put all these things together, makes you wonder.

I have added links here you can check out on the Jade Helm topic.

https://www.youtube.com/watch?v=Q3tc4-qKvzw

https://www.youtube.com/watch?v=wGOuzeeSzUg

https://www.youtube.com/watch?v=K4310XOz4tc

https://en.wikipedia.org/wiki/Jade_Helm_15_conspiracy_theories

https://www.youtube.com/watch?v=l3IhN7itG6Y

https://www.youtube.com/watch?v=Dhgrgf9sYK8

https://www.youtube.com/watch?v=7i1F8rL7rSk

https://www.youtube.com/watch?v=4L1IFoLO8f0

https://www.youtube.com/watch?v=UusMk7JNmQs

https://www.youtube.com/watch?v=1zJ4DJOt5T0

Is America getting off Track?

I am hoping that America will wake up and see this is not the path to freedom, but to a state of never ending fear. To a state of no more choices, where we once grew up and played, will seize to exist.

This next war may be the bloodiest as it will be more than just over land, it will be over your total freedom. How much of this is real I do not truly know, but I think it is interesting that when you connect all the dots we will see a picture we probably will not like.

America has fallen before with the great depression, but we rose back up. Let's protect our country before it is too late. If you are ready we will move on to our next story, as Deception, shadows of truth continues.

TWIN TOWERS/911

On a warm Fall day in New York, on September 11, 2001, the world suddenly stopped as video was shown and the news across this country of what could only be seen as unimaginable.

One of the Twin Towers was struck by a plane as people watched in shock and disbelief from below and afar. The blue sky, from above, suddenly releases a black plume, as it towers above the city. As more and more eyes are drawn on this treacherous disaster, while another plane carrying innocent passengers, like the one before is seen flying towards the second Twin Tower. As though it were all being done in slow motion, as it too collides, into the side of the second tower. Suddenly both towers are engulfed in flames. Now America is on high alert as even a simpleton knew this was no accident.

The news reported four planes were unaccounted for as America is ordered to land all private and commercial planes.

Suddenly, the Pentagon is struck as a plane hit there as well, leaving its footprint on the outside of the Pentagon, as more are killed and destruction spreads. Three of the four planes have now been accounted for as finally, the fourth is found to have crashed in a field near the Diamond T. mine in Stoneycreek , Township Summerset county in Pennsylvania. Luckily, the ones who died on that plane, gave their lives to save many more that would have been harmed. Though the intensions of the hijackers is unknown, it is thought they were looking to target either the White House, or the Capitol Building. Those that died that day were all victims and heroes to us all.

The 9/11 conspiracies started to rise. As more questions were being asked, the more suspicious the answers would become. So as we take a look at this tragic event keep an open mind.

I am going to start this a little differently, as we look at Building Seven. It was the third building that was destroyed, yet few knew of its destruction till late. The government stated the building collapsed due to fire. They state it was the furniture that created this building to weaken and fall. The government later acknowledged that the building collapsed at the rate of freefall.

Jonathan Barnett, PhD Fire Protection Engineer stated, "We are surprised it collapsed. We being the team that investigated what had occurred. There was some damage that occurred from the debris that hit it from tower one, but the damage was certainly not the same scope or magnitude caused by the aircraft that hit towers one and two."

Building Seven, fell seven hours after the Twin Towers collapsed. It collapsed in under seven seconds Luckily, no one was inside the building. Did we get lucky and miraculously escape, or was it calculated as we made time to get everyone out before we ourselves, created the explosion and conclusion to Tower Seven?

William Rice, P.E. Civil Structural Engineer and Engineering Professor at Vermont Technical College stated, "The only way a building can accelerate as it collapses, is having pre-engineered, precisely timed, precisely placed explosions, making this a controlled demolition."

Roland Angel, P.E. Civil Structural Engineer stated, "This is high school physics."

Craig Bartmer, is a former NYPD First Responder. He was there at ground zero. He stated he heard no sounds of cracking noises you would expect to hear from a building that was getting ready to fall. He also stated he thought he would know the sound of an explosion if he heard one. He stated other eye witnesses claimed to have heard explosions as well.

Irwin Cantor, WTC7(World Trade Center 7) Engineer of Record stated, "It was a good building, it was soundly designed. It would still be standing if not for 9/11 and it was state of the art at the time." We have two groups of people that are presenting two different stories. It is important to remember this, as we continue looking for a true motive, or emotive as it is presented to us by our leaders and specialists.

Michael Donly, Structural Engineer, Leslie Young, Architect, and William Brinner, Architect, along with 1400 other Architects and Engineers, found the governments conclusion to be physically impossible.

Why should we not believe these people who have gone through years of schooling and training? Why should we trust the other group and who is this other group? It is those that are political, the ones we all elected to represent us, we the people. The one's we look to for answers in times of turmoil. We Americans still believe that our Government is there to work for us, and not us for them. It does not mean it is perfect or that we trust all politicians. In fact most politicians seem to either be corrupt or their hands are kept tied till they themselves fall victim to corruption.

The media also plays into how we are informed. We watch talk shows like the View who sound off, trying to create points that should be looked at in an unbiased manner. On this video we see Elizabeth Hasselbeck and Rosie O'Donnell who seem a bit heated as they talk about what we have just mentioned.

Elizabeth states on the show, "Do you believe the government had anything to do with 9/11? Do you believe in conspiracy in terms of the attack on 9/11?" Rosie O'Donnell stated, " No, but I do believe this is the first time fire has ever melted steel." Rosie O' Donnell encouraged them to bring the specialists on who have said it is physically impossible for steel to be melted by fire. Elizabeth seemed defensive as she asked, "Who do you think is responsible for that?"

While it is important to know who is responsible, it is just as important to look at the facts and evidence as well. In any criminal case you look at motive, means, and opportunity. These are just more tools we can use while we evaluate all this information.

Daniel Barnum, FAIA (The American Institute of Architect) is a high rise architect. He says himself looking at the fires in Building Seven, that they weren't even raging. He said it couldn't happen.

> ### NIST NCSTAR 1A
> Federal Building and Fire and Safety Investigation of the World Trade Center Disaster. Final Report on the Collapse of the World Trade Center Building 7.
>
> **The draft for public comment.**

Why does a final report say specifically, (draft for public comment)? To me a report is a report, whether it is made public or not. This investigation was completed by The National Institute of Standards and Technology United States Department of Commerce. It took three years. Shyam Sunder, NIST WTC lead investigator states they did studies showing where for the first time a building could collapse by fire induced progressive collapse. However looking at the computed generated model on the video, it still shows it coming down from one side before the other. The videos of Building Seven all show it coming down in a very even manner. They state there was a break in the city's water main keeping the sprinkler system from working on the lower floors.

They state there were no witnesses to the explosions and none were picked up from audio tracks or tapes. On this video they show us multiple tracks from different locations that very distinctly let you hear explosions. There are witnesses too, yet they said they had none?

They show a reporter, her name is Ashleigh Banfield. When she is talking to one lady with a child she acts surprised as the explosions erupts, she says, " This is it." She says that before the building starts to fall? Before this event she reports that she has heard from several different officers that Building Seven is going to go down next.

Once again I point out means, motive and opportunity. The means is the media, it is able to reach millions of people. Motive is to get the American people furious with those that attacked our people, our land, and our beliefs. Opportunity, we already have two buildings down with total chaos, as all are confused. What better time than to incorporate one more blast.

While I would like to comment on Brian Williams, the News Anchorman, I have decided anything he reports can no longer be substantiated, as he has lied to the American people before, as I had written in my Changing America books.

David Rastuccio, NYC Fire Dept. Lt. confirmed it was Building Seven that fell and he stated he heard it was unstable and eventually it would come down on its own or would be taken down.

When the smoke clears who will be blamed?

Deception through the media, is always plausible, whether direct on their part, or from outside sources with no true knowledge of intent.

Supposedly NIST was never published by a peer reviewed publication. Is this normal practice? Is there a reason that the NIST would not want to publish in a manner that could validate its own findings? Using motive, means and opportunity again, we see that the motive for not doing so would cause more questions if they were hiding something. Means is that they want us to believe that the NIST is going to be fair and impartial and is a recognized professional organization. The last being opportunity, here they have the ability to validate their findings, yet choose not to do so.

They mention whether this was planned and if so was it planned ahead of the 9/11 attacks? Was it part of the attack itself? If this was something they did on the spur of the moment, could it have even been done with the fires going on as they were?

These are just some of the questions that we Americans want to know as we try and figure out what really happened. Geraldo Rivera was reporting outside on the mystery of World Trade Center Building Seven, when a bunch of protesters were yelling "Inside Job." He turned and looked at them and said, "get a life."

What if they were right? How does the news media report this, knowing we, or should I say they, were wrong and didn't look in to it more? I like Geraldo, but what is the purpose of reporting the news if you don't report it fairly, with unbiased prejudice?

I will say Geraldo Rivera did follow up and ask questions, when I thought at first he would not. Even he admitted to giving it a second look after the families of 9/11 and the Architects raised concerns.

Clouded in mystery

The Twin Towers scream for justice, as NIST goes silent.

We need to remember while we talk about 9/11, that it is not just about three buildings that have been destroyed, but thousands of lives from the victims to their families and to every American that had to view this horrific event.

America was attacked, but by whom? Americans have a right to know and to protect their country at any cost, whether foreign, or domestic.

It is time to come back around to the Twin Towers as we look at more evidence that leaves us wondering. Fire fighters that had come out of the towers said there was a secondary explosion. That the lobby just collapsed. How is this possible when the explosion from the plane was clear up near the top? The fireman said there was a third explosion as well.

One of the rescuers stated, "there was no fire in the lobby, just looked like a bomb went off in the lobby."

William Rodriguez was a janitor that was working in one of the towers the day of the event he was in basement one. He stated, "when I heard the explosion it pushed us upwards in the air." He then mentioned seconds later hearing a bang and explosion from the plane hitting the side of the building up above.

I'm not sure if this will be mentioned later but as the cameras scan towards the Twin Towers and we see the first plane hit I caught a glimpse of a fireman standing around on the street with another fireman. Were these fire fighters responding to a previous fire that was called, or to this horrific event? It is interesting how the camera seemed to know where to look right before the plane crashed. The next question after looking at the tape, is a passenger plane is no small vehicle. So why do we not see more of it as we watch the explosion? Even if it is a blur you would expect to see more than a dot, round, or projectile. To me that seemed odd as I watched the video. I also looked at where the impact was at first so as to get the correct side of the building.

This way no one could say the plane was hidden due to the building itself. On the video Jeff King, MIT Engineer Research Scientist, had talked with someone who was a retired Corp of Engineers, they said it was a clear sign of demolition, as they mentioned squibs were seen coming out other windows leaving puffs of smoke from below.

They talk about the evidence being destroyed and preventing the investigation by choosing who does the investigation. They mention about the fires being extremely hot, yet the experts statement was, it's not that hot.

Robert Podolsky, M.S. Physicist / Engineer stated the fire had to be burning at 750 degrees Fahrenheit. He mentioned you could hold that fire under a steel beam forever and not bend the steel.

Were these three buildings destroyed not by planes and fire, but explosives? I think America wants, needs, and deserves an answer for every question raised about this incident.

In order to stop conspiracies and deception, all must reveal the truth. Shadows of truth will remain till we can make certain all questions that are asked are not just given and answered, but given with a realistic answer, that is believable to the majority.

A picture is worth a thousand words so what is a video worth? I am sure much more, as you watch these videos and see with your own eyes.

There are eye witnesses that say they saw molten steel running down the channels. They described it like lava. In the video you can see firsthand, that is what is happening. To create steel to melt the temperature needs to be at least 2700 degrees Fahrenheit, jet fuel which is basically kerosene burns at less than 1600 degrees Fahrenheit. I am only repeating what the experts are saying.

There is also the evidence that is in the iron rich sphere, in the ruble, and the medal pouring out the side of the towers.

Gery Warner, P.E. Mechanical Engineer, stated what he saw pouring out of the towers was molten iron due to the color. He explained the difference from his experience in the field as he stated, "we turned aluminum oxide into aluminum. Molten aluminum is silver, it's not yellow it's silver."

They talk about when they are cleaning up the after math it was still so hot, if they put water on it, you would create so much steam no one would be able to see what they were doing. They mentioned there were fires with temperatures of 2000 degrees below the ground.

They talk about the cloud of smoke itself, that it occurs in only two type of situations naturally, one being volcanic eruptions where it is exploded putting particles into the air, the other is called trevinity currents which occur on the edges of continental shelves where mud or sediment . They call the clouds pyroclastic, which to me stands for only one thing, if not volcanic material then manmade explosives.

The Twin Towers were designed to withstand the hit of a 707 jet liner, which at the time was the biggest plane we had. The professionals state that it would, or should been able to withstand the hit and compared it to a pencil being poked through a screen window. They mentioned it would have done very little damage.

The ENR (Engineering News Record) April 2, 1964 stated in their paper, "Live loads on these columns can be increased more than 2,000% before failure occurs."

David Childs, Architect of the new Freedom Tower and WTC 7 high-rise stated, "Never in the history of a steel structure building has a steel structured building ever fallen down for reasons of fire."

We have gone over the destructions of the buildings, as we listen to experts give their expert opinions. We have listened to those in the political arena give their opinions, as well. The question is, who do you believe and why?

You have much of the evidence and you have history that speaks as well. While you look at everything be open minded to both sides. For it is only the gullible that can be deceived.

As we continue on with the videos of the plane, that were, or were not there, remember the stories before, as all is not always as it appears to be. It happens to be a tragic event that many wish could have been avoided, but it will take the truth to not only find out, but to change any future events that could be headed our way.

When we look at the videos of the planes hitting the Twin Towers, you have to look at every angle. As we look at the videos you see the tip of the nose from the plane, clear up to the wing disappear before an explosion. You then see a plane fly away from the towers as well. They show one clip where there is a crane and the plane appears in front of part of the crane. To me you can't have the plane in two different spots.

They show the exit side of the building yet no hole where the plane should have left some type of imprint. They compare a truck hitting a cement wall then show a truck being driven straight through a jet liner. It totally demolished the plane. The cement wall though beat the truck.

There is one clip they talk about the nose of the plane. They show you a clip of what looks to be the nose of the plane coming through the backside of the building. If this is what they want us to believe then why is the nose still in that good of shape?

I love watching Fox News and enjoy most of the reporters. Sean Hannity, who I enjoy listening too, said on the show, "this was not an inside job, we can see the planes, the planes hit the building, it wasn't a controlled demolition and the buildings came down. It is just beyond bizarre, that he believes it, but he is entitled to. But he doesn't have a right to teach our students in a classroom, it's not a right."

Do the reporters have a right to report information knowing it is false?

Do the reporters collect their own information on what happens, or do they get their information second hand? I am no professional reporter, but I am an American that wants to discuss issues that raise concerns, along with all the American people, who feel they are just not being told everything.

They mentioned that people on the streets of New York stated they saw no markings on the side of the plane that hit the tower and some said it was gray or black. They mentioned it was a military plane with no windows on the side of the plane where passengers would have window viewing.

One thing we need to keep in mind is after an event happens, especially, one involving the word conspiracy the evidence is whisked away, people disappear, or die. It might just be coincidence, or maybe not.

Why did they destroy the steel structures instead of keep them so as to try and figure out what really happened? With many accidents they salvage what they can and try to reconstruct it as much as possible. Why did it take 3 years to get it all put together? Was it to give them enough time to create a model that could be closely simulated to look like what had happened?

On the News channel, Chopper 4 Live you can see in the video a missile or small plane approaching in a missile type manner as it hit the tower creating a horrific explosion. This was not a large jet liner, but a small plane or missile. Why should we not look at this, or question this event when the object is clearly visible, enough to know it was not a jet liner.

It is good to question all things and do so with an open mind. God knows what happened, so if a conspiracy has been done, it's no longer a secret.

What is interesting is that there were lots of video clips and drawings before 9/11 that make it seem as though it had already happened, or was known ahead of time it would happen. I have always maintained what means nothing today may mean everything tomorrow.

As we continue on with the Pentagon crash think about the statement above.

Pentagon on 9/11

War has reached our borders, while the enemy is still to be defined.

As the whole world turned on television and tuned into the 9/11 WTC catastrophe, another was about to explode. The Pentagon comes under an aerial assault that demolishes a section of the Pentagon and causes havoc that leaves Americans on edge, as we try to find out who is behind these sinister plots of doom.

The computer generated animation, shows the path of the plane and the destruction it left behind. Lamp pole one, was struck from Flight 77's right wing as the pole hit a taxi. Lamp pole two is struck by left wing as it continues toward the Pentagon. A total of five poles before it crashes into the side of the Pentagon.

Again many say it was a missile that hit the building and not a plane. They mention they had war games going on at the time of the attack, which prevented the slow response of fighter jets to intercept.

They mention Operation North Woods, a pretext to justify military intervention in Cuba. It was a mission developed by the Joint Chief of Staff. The Operation dictated swapping commercial aircrafts once airborne with drones and shooting them out of the sky. Using this action to blame Cuba in order to justify a military strike, gaining public and congressional support.

There is data that shows flight UA93 still airborne, as well as N612 UA, after which supposedly it had struck the South tower. Why is this data not accepted? What would be the reason for them being shown still in flight, if they had already crashed? Maybe I am just misunderstanding the information?

UA93 was shown still airborne and just south of the impact crater, according to ATC transcripts. AKARS DATA, a device used to communicate with aircraft, shows UA175 still airborne in Western Pennsylvania. This was approximately twenty minutes after the reported crash.

According to a Radar Specialist and Electrical Engineer it is impossible, if the flight crashed in to the tower, it could not have then transmitted like it did.

The AKARS DATA reports the closest station to and from an aircraft. AKARS DATA shows it had transmitted from Harrisburg and Pittsburg Pennsylvania, when according to the official report it should have come from those in New York.

Facts that wave conspiracy, fraud, and deception.
- War games operating during the terrorist attacks.
- Aircraft exceeding their maximum operating limits by more than 130 to 150 knots.
- Inaccurate positions of aircraft reports.
- False aircraft target reports.
- Air craft conversing, flying virtually information with, then diverging from 9/11 reported aircraft.
- Fighter jets launched in the wrong direction.
- Aircraft still airborne after the alleged crash.
- Poor communications and phones not working,

Should these not matter to us? Are these just coincidences? Why do we look away from the professionals and experts that have years of knowledge and experiences?

There are those that say they saw planes crash into the buildings, how is this possible if there were no planes? There is talk of a holographic projector, which displays a three dimensional image in a desired location. We have mastered many things in our lifetime, is not a holographic projector, not out of this realm? We communicate on wireless phones, we have traveled to the moon, we can face-time now as we look at each other from across the world. Holographic has been around a long time in many different variations, namely Hollywood.

The television series The Lone Gunman released March 2001, six months before 9/11 showed a plane being controlled from the ground and targeting the World Trade Center. What are the odds of that? If you start watching television programs closer you will also see how quick the media slash Hollywood get these events into their programs and series with miraculous timing?

They mention there is no wreckage of planes in the Twin Towers. If this is true then a holographic image could explain why some saw a plane.

If you look at the evidence, it will either add up, or it won't. The problem with evidence is sometimes it gets contaminated. Now you have to decide who contaminated it and why? This comes back to the three things I had mentioned earlier, motive means, and opportunity. You have to figure out why it happened, who could have done it, and if others knew or were involved.

Look at evidence like a puzzle when the pieces are connected a picture appears making more sense.

Look at these links and make your own assumptions as you view everything individually and openly trying not to be persuaded until all the evidence has been presented.

https://www.youtube.com/watch?v=4Nmj6t51Wz8

https://www.youtube.com/watch?v=IL8cJWyOxWQ

https://www.youtube.com/watch?v=cHHghW4Pg5k

https://www.youtube.com/watch?v=YVDdjLQkUV8

https://www.youtube.com/watch?v=-Laaq44SDgg

https://www.youtube.com/watch?v=YQBlv7sZGVE

There are many, many, more links, check them out as you search for the truth, while you explore what seems to be unimaginable, or unfathomable, as someone like Gene Rosen from Connecticut would say.

I want to believe in my government, rather than them manipulate me along with other Americans. If you are ready, we will move on to our next story, as Deception, shadows of truth continues.

WACO SIEGE

On February 28, 1993 outside a small town known as Waco, Texas, a standoff between ATF (Bureau of Alcohol Tobacco and Firearms) agents and a small community called the Branch Davidians becomes more than heated, as everyone watches from a far and near.

The ATF state they are there to arrest David Koresh and had been informed of weapons and a possible meth lab. The incident began when the ATF attempted to raid the ranch and intense gunfire erupted killing six Branch Davidians and four Federal agents.

Due to the unsuccessful raid of the compound, the siege initiated by the ATF now becomes a televised standoff, watched by everyone, between the two groups lasting fifty one days.

Once again conspiracy flies its flag, as questions arise covering the televised event seen by all.

The Branch Davidians were a religious group, but were also known as survivalists. They bought weapons for self defense and stored food items to sustain themselves.

Wally Kennett , one of the Branch Davidians stated that, members who were booted out for immoral behaviors, cooked up the stories of child molestation and weapons violations. That between these people and the ATF, and FBI (Federal Bureau of Investigations) they had just cause.

They mentioned that the Branch Davidians were targeted due to their stock piling of weapons by both ATF, and the FBI. The ATF was originally established to collect taxes for the US Treasury Department, today their mission is that of disarming American civilian population. Making Waco 's Branch Davidians their target for extermination.

So as we look at this raid we have to look at it as what was their true objective?

Catherine Matteson stated she had heard three helicopters, confirming the number as she looked out the window. It was at that time she viewed them with guns shooting at them, from above in the helicopters. She was reported to have said the ATF had fired the first shots She stated, "I was in the back of the building, that's where my room was and they were firing towards David's room. They turned I fell to the floor because, I could see those bullets could of hit me if I was standing.

They went to the front of the building and by the time they got to the front they were firing again, and so all of the others were firing."

Annetta Richards testimony was nearly identical to that of Catherine Matteson who stated, "I was upstairs getting ready for worship and I heard noise like a helicopter, I heard guns start firing, bullets start coming in from every direction." She heard someone tell her to get down and she saw a baby being held by a little girl. She took the baby to help shield the baby from bullets.

These stories were confirmed by Dr. Bruce Perry Psychologist. Using information from one of the children that had left the Branch Davidians that evening.

One of the ATF agents stated, "The problem wasn't that we were out planned, it was that we were out gunned."

Ron Cole, an independent investigator interviewed eye witnesses and did his own research. Coming up with one conclusion, using a scaled model of the ranch he showed the events as they were described to him.

He mentioned that the people that were in a position to see the helicopters said they fired first. Where those that were in front of the center, could hear the helicopters, but couldn't see them, but did see the agents exiting the cattle trailers. It was those in the cattle trailer that said the first shots came from the front.

Ron Cole stated, "This is why it seems to me, that shots were fired from agents at the front and from the helicopters within seconds of each other. Which means there would not have been enough time for some emergency code word to have been used, or for someone else to have fired the first shot that would have initiated simultaneous fire from the ground and from the air within seconds of each other. That indicates to me that this was planned in advance. That it was a frontal assault from the ground and air support coming in from the back, simultaneous preplanned attack."

David Koresh stated he opened the door yelling out at the ATF agents, "go away there are women and children here, let's talk. Then shots started firing and I shut the door."

Looking at the video you see ATF agents on one side as they're shooting at the building, no rounds appear to be seen being fired back hitting the ground, vehicles, or agents, with the exception of one agent who shoots himself while trying to retrieve his gun from his holster as he's traveling up the ladder.

The agents on the roof are now in harm's way as they try to enter the inside of the building while shots are being fired from the front and supposedly shots are being fired from inside. Now three enter through a window while a fourth covers for them. Suddenly the fourth pulls the curtain back tosses in a canister of smoke, or a concussion grenade while three of his own members are inside this very same room?

You can see shots from inside being fired outside as you see holes appear on the outer wall and the ATF agent fall backwards as he is struck in the helmet. He did not sustain any injuries, and was able to climb back down on his own. The shots had to have come from inside the building or from the helicopters as they were on the second story and the shots appeared more straight.

Just looking at what we have covered so far you have to ask was this really about arresting David Koresh? Have you ever seen law enforcement go into a hostage crisis and not at least attempt to first start with negotiations, especially where there are women and children involved? If they said they attempted to, then who was the hostage negotiator?

If the crisis was such it needed addressed with a tactical team trained in these situations, then why did it take fifty one days, tanks, helicopters and the complete annihilation of the buildings and vehicles? Could it had been for the purpose of television exposure and a country of witnesses to see what others wanted us to see through their carefully orchestrated eyes? Was this an arrest that went bad? Was it all planned? Did all these people really die?

This is about conspiracies, lies, and deception. As we continue on here with another theory, that this was all staged by Bill Clinton himself, keep an open mind as we go through more interesting evidence. Remember the Clinton name has been brought up in many other scandals putting his credibility out there for each to make their own conclusion, as we are our own judges.

Dick Morris, Former Clinton Advisor discussed on FOX News that Timothy McVeigh's motivation with the Oklahoma bombing was due to the Waco siege. Dick Morris mentioned Bill Clinton orchestrating the takeover, and that he was so ashamed of the takeover he was not going to appoint Janet Reno to a second term as Attorney General of the United States. Janet Reno told him in a meeting right before the inauguration day, "If you don't appoint me I am going to tell the truth about Waco."

Dick Morris told that, "Clinton stated I could not, not appoint Reno, because she would have turned on me with Waco. That was the phrase he used."

According to the Waco Tribune-Herald's, the ATF had planned their raid for Monday March 1, 1993, code named *Showtime*. It was then moved up a day to February 28,1993 in response to the Tribune's release of a series of articles, named Sinful Messiah.

The paper states they were asked by the ATF not to publish the Sinful Messiah articles and had three meetings set up beginning February 1st regarding the delay of publication. The Tribune was first told by the ATF, that the raid would take place on February 22nd and then soon changed to March 1stand finally to an indefinite date.

The ATF attempted to execute their search warrant on a Sunday morning, February 28, 1993. The advantage of a surprise was lost, when a reporter from KWXT TV showed up and asked for directions from a US Postal worker, who just happened to be David Koresh's brother-in-law.

At approximately five o'clock in the morning seventy six agents assembled at Fort Hood, for the drive to Bellmead Civic Center which was the staging area. They then drove in an eighty vehicle convoy stretching over a mile with a cattle car at each end.

At 9:45am the agents move in as the gun battle begins. Three minutes later one of the Branch Davidian members, Wayne Martin, an attorney calls 911.

At 11:30 am a cease fire is called, four and a half hours later at 4:00pm the first message from David Koresh is heard over KLRD Radio station, in Texas.

They mention the death certificates as they show on line only six people listed that died on February 28, 2014 in McLennan county Texas. These names as shown were, Alma K. Brown, W.J. Connaway, Bronson Cravy, Raymond C. Durham, Ruth G. McGuire, and Myrtice A. Watson.

They mentioned three agents reached David Koresh's window as they came under fire. One agent was killed, while another was wounded. The third agent joined members of his team outside the alleged arms room. On video you see one agent breaking the glass throwing in a grenade of some sort, whether concussion or smoke. Soon you see three of four agents enter the room while the fourth agent remains outside. Then you see the video must have been cut as it shows the last agent up by the window as he tosses some type of grenade in the same room that his team members had earlier entered.

Due to the cut it is hard to tell how much time had elapsed from the time his team had entered the room. You may assume he thinks all the members of his team are dead, or maybe he is there to take out his team and blame the Branch Davidians.

Who's team is he on?

Why would he have to clear a room that was just cleared, unless his team mates were dead and it was over taken again by the Branch Davidians? Once he tosses a canister inside he precedes to shoot without looking to see if those were his own members he was shooting at.

So as we go back to the death certificates, we see six names. Were any of these names associated with either side? According to the video the ones who died were, Steve Willis, Robert Williams, Todd Mc Keehan, and Conway LeBleu, along with one unknown, all agents. The ones on the other side associated with the Branch Davidians that were killed were, Winston Blake, Peter Gent, Peter Hipsman, Perry Jones, and Jaydean Wendell.

We have ten names here of people who died yet it only shows up as six on the website? The names do not match either side. There was Michael Schroeder who was shot to death by agents after they said he allegedly shot at them. His body laid in a ravine for five days 300 ft. from Mount Carmel. He was shot seven times as he was trying to return home to the compound. Two others that were with Michael were arrested and taken into custody.

I have both military and law enforcement training, when you watch the officers shooting from behind the vehicles I notice a couple red flags. First I would not let one of my own get behind me as he uses me for a shield. Each officer should be using independent cover while not putting their own people at risk. The second thing is when you watch the videos you will see guns being fired by other agents right beside their heads, near their ears. To me this just displays fake, or inexperienced officers.

We talked about those that died but we did not even include the women and children and those inside the building, that number is said to be near seventy nine. What happened to all the bodies? Were all the bodies accounted for?

The ATF claimed that the fires that consumed everyone was committed by the Branch Davidians themselves, calling it a mass suicide. They do not mention that there is video that shows otherwise.

You can see from tanks as they back out of the walls, flames coming from the tanks themselves. It appears as though it's a giant flamethrower on the end of the tanks. There was said to be video of the assault from the front as David Koresh mentioned seeing cameras. Where are these videos? David Hardy, Attorney, Investigator stated, "The agency claimed there were three, or four cameras pointed at the front of the building that saw everything that happened that day. They claim they can't find a single one of them, every one of those video tapes vanished." In addition to the missing video tapes, the ATF activity log transcripts also disappeared. There are notes torn out of the surveillance log that can't be accounted for.

Joe Turner, Branch Davidian Criminal Defense Attorney stated the ATF had a plan. If the dogs came up to attack them they were to shoot the dogs. He stated an ATF agent testified that they did shoot the dogs. In the video you see a row of dogs laying there dead. You also see a bunch of go-carts lined up in a row outside underneath where the two ladders were placed.

The ATF agent on the video stated we are a Law Enforcement agency we don't fire through walls indiscriminately, yet the video shows that to be just the case. Officers shooting pistols from a distance with no true intent of accuracy.

Was this shooting sponsored by Wal-Mart?

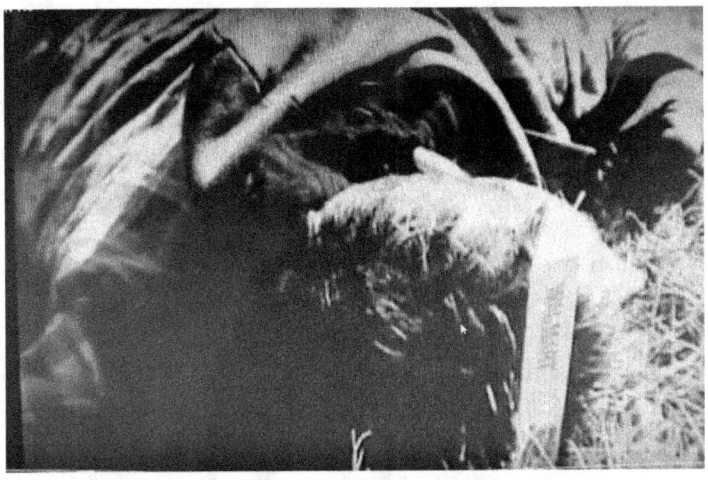

It is very odd that a stick used to mark the area where Michael Schroeder's body lay, has Wal-Mart on it? To some they would think it was just a stick that was convenient. To me though, it made me think back to Jade Helm. It is very possible it means nothing, but then again Shadows of truth leaves no stone unturned, and no sign ignored. They showed his stocking cap with a hole in it yet on the video I see no blood? His body was cremated before any autopsy was able to be done, per his family's request.

They were able to save twenty one children from the youngest being five months old to the oldest being twelve years old. Some adults were rescued along with the children. The children were handed over to Texas Social Services. While some lives were saved others like Michael Schroeder were not.

Officials stated upon the arrival of the tanks that these tanks would not be armed and they were not there to assault the compound. That these tanks were for defensive purposes only.

As I watch one of these videos you get to hear the dialogue between Steve Schneider, a Branch Davidian and an FBI Negotiator. It appears to me that the FBI had decided they want no survivors or witnesses. I got that impression from the following conversation.

FBI Negotiator: "There's been a change, the tactical people have changed the situation and for security reasons, and for safety reasons, no one is now authorized to come out of there for any reason. What they are telling me is that if anybody does, they're going to be dealt with in such a fashion that the people will have to, um, retreat back to the compound."

Steve: "What? I... I'm missing what you're saying now. Are you saying... make it as plain as possible."

FBI Negotiator: "The patience of the bosses is no longer where it was earlier."

Steve: "Ok."

FBI Negotiator: "In this, in this."

Steve: "I'm about ready to... Listen to me now Henry, I don't really care about your bosses. When you tell me one thing, or you tell us that is ok, and this Bradley comes up and says something contrary to what you are, you tell your bosses to get their butts together, you hear me?"

The Justice Department intervened, preventing FBI Director William Sessions from boarding a plane to fly down to Waco to assist with the crisis, to conduct face to face negotiations with David Koresh. It was the government officials in Washington DC., Who prevented this from happening.

The three agents that entered through the window were killed, all three were Bill Clintons bodyguards during his Presidential campaign. Does this not smell like Washington? Why are there three bodyguards going into a building that the ATF are responsible for? Were these agents trained in the same manner? Was this a hit on those bodyguards and then covered up using a prefabricated story, called Waco? The fourth agent was killed that day before the shooting started, as he exited the cattle car.

It is something to look at. How many people have died of suspicious deaths that were connected to The Clintons?

When we look at what the true intentions were, we have to think it was not to arrest David Koresh, but to destroy the compound. They surrounded the compound, then drove tanks over their vehicles using military might. They used the tanks to crush the stairs and exits keeping everyone trapped inside the building. The negotiator again told everyone they could not leave. They used the helicopters to get a better advantage point as they shot indiscriminately at all that were inside the building. There was no age discrimination, all were considered hostile, even the women and children.

Is it not their job to get everyone out of the building in a peaceful manner, saving lives while preventing more casualties? Why would they not want them to surrender, unless they feared consequential retaliation from witnesses and their superiors?

During the standoff they cut power to the building depriving them of heat, light, and water. They tried tactics of sleep deprivation, where they called making the phone ring constantly. They played revelry, sounding of trumpets and other sound effects. None of these tactics worked. Were these the reasons things went off kilter? Had they tried everything they could think of?

On one of the videos you see what appears to be an officer rescuing someone from the burning building. That agent was Jim McGee, who stated he saw a woman come out and then head back in. He stated he put his weapon down running in after her pulling her to safety where minutes later the building she had tried to enter collapsed.

We may never know the truth about Waco but there is a lot of conflicting stories that seem to lead to conspiracies and cover ups. Why did the FBI Negotiator tell those inside the building not to come out. When on another interview an FBI Negotiator stated he pleaded for them to leave the building?

Who was really in charge that day, and what about President Clinton's three bodyguards that died inside the building. Could they have been killed by friendly fire? Were they secretly assassinated? Where are the death records for all those who died near eighty people in all.

Steve Schneider mentioned the name Henry during the negotiation. On the other video clip Byron Sage, an FBI Negotiator stated he had talked with Steve Schneider. So were there more than one negotiator? Which would make sense as it took fifty one days, but the question why two different sets of instructions? You would think they would communicate with each other, always looking at the end goal of getting them all out safely.

Here are some more links that you can watch on YouTube. I hope you are enjoying the information I am bringing to you. I know most of it seems gloomy, but most Conspiracies are.

Links on Waco

https://www.youtube.com/watch?v=xsDBAixXJdM

https://www.youtube.com/watch?v=8xRaJ5QA1kk

https://www.youtube.com/watch?v=s3CGyH5ftdE

https://en.wikipedia.org/wiki/Waco_siege

https://www.youtube.com/watch?v=XreYBolUn7s

https://www.youtube.com/watch?v=zpeF2VXWVlk

https://www.youtube.com/watch?v=RrJewJPyptk

If you are ready, we will move on to our next story, as Deception, shadows of truth continues.

Oklahoma City, Oklahoma Bombing

As we continue on we move to April 19, 1995 in Oklahoma City, Oklahoma, at 9am. An explosion went off at the Alfred P. Murrah Federal Building creating a blast that was felt for miles in all directions.

Bomb sniffing dogs were brought in and everything was put on hold when they were alerted to two, or three more bombs. The news on NBC stated they had been informed a few bombs had been defused already. After the blast and more bombs were found, the first responders were then ordered away from the building for nearly an hour and a half before they could resume rescuing people.

Kent Ogle reported the Bio medical science building, on the South side of the children's hospital, was being evacuated as well due to bomb threats. There were twelve children being treated at the trauma center ranging from two months old up to eighteen years old. There was an eighteen month old baby with burns over fifty five percent of his or her body. There is currently sixty five adults that have been, or are being treated as well.

When all was said and done 168 people were dead and 680 more were injured. There were 324 buildings in a sixteen block radius that were destroyed, or damaged. There were eighty six cars that had been burned, leaving Oklahoma City, Oklahoma with over 652 million dollars worth of damage.

America was on high alert, as we all sat in disbelief shocked by what had just happened.

The Federal Emergency Management Agency (FEMA) activated eleven of its Urban Search and Rescue Task Forces, consisting of 665 rescue workers who assisted in rescue and recovery operations.

Within ninety minutes after the explosion, Timothy McVeigh was stopped by Oklahoma State Trooper, Charlie Hanger. He pulled him over for driving without a license plate and was arrested for illegal weapons possession. Forensic evidence quickly linked Timothy McVeigh and Terry Nichols to the bombing. Both were arrested and within days, charged with the Oklahoma City bombing. They also identified two other accomplices, Michael and Lori Fortier who had prior knowledge of the attack.

Timothy McVeigh was identified as a Gulf War Veteran and part of a militia movement sympathizer. He was being accused of renting a Ryder truck and filling it full of explosives and detonating it in front of the Alfred P. Murrah Federal Building.

Terry Nichols was identified as his co-conspirator and assisted in the bomb preparation. They stated that Terry was motivated by hatred towards the Federal government's handling of the Waco siege, and the Ruby Ridge incident that we will get into later.

The official investigation was named, (OKBOMB) The FBI conducted 28,000 interviews, they collected approximately one billion pieces of information. Timothy McVeigh was executed by lethal injection on June 11, 2001.

Terry Nichols was sentenced to life in prison in 2004. Michael and Lori Fortier testified against the other two and Michael was sentenced to twelve years in prison, while Lori received immunity for her testimony.

As we go back looking at the event that clouded Americas vision, through chaos, and or calculated steps to deceive all America with intentional misperception. Remember keep an open mind

America is now being attacked by our own people, by Americans who say they are not a cult, or fanatics, but by those who say they are our neighbors and sheriffs, by those that work on our vehicles. Timothy McVeigh according to the official report bombed the Alfred P. Murrah Federal Building due to the Federal Government's handling of the Waco siege two years earlier, however others believe it goes deeper. There are some that believe it is those on the far right that have longed to blow up a Federal Building, using this as a staging for a revolutionary attack on the government.

A plot to blow up the Murrah building began in 1983 by a group known as the CSA (Covenant Sword and Arm of the Lord), located in rural Arkansas. In the early 1970's the CSA began as a group of religious separatists known as the Zarephath Horeb church. They were just your typical young people who wanted to live a peaceful life, learn about God and raise their families away from violence. In 1978 things changed the group then started to believe that judgment day was near and a major shift in the group took place. The organization then began to stockpile food and weapons and train for survival.

They were preparing for Armageddon and isolated themselves from society. They then split in to Christian identity, which preaches that the true lineage of God is made up of Arians and White people.

Kerry Noble a former member of the CSA, stated "This is where our downfall began." They saw the Jews as the liberal descendants of the devil, they went from a simple religious community to transforming into soldiers of God, changing their name from Zarephath Horeb church, to Covenant Sword and Arm of the Lord.

They constructed a city, a compound for elite military training for various racist, anti government, and fascist groups around the country. They had machine guns, grenades, and silencers.

In 1983 an event takes place, Gordon Wendall Kahl is on the run for tax evasion when law enforcement officers try to apprehend him and are killed. Gordon Kahl leads them on a cross country chase where he is tracked down in Northern Arkansas and killed in a violent shoot out. He is then seen as a martyr, as a true patriot.

This group seen this as near their area. They said whatever the government did to them they would do double to seven times. Just happens a Jewish center is bombed in Bloomington, Indiana in 1983.

Kerry Noble mentioned they met a man by the name of Richard Wayne Schnell He was the one who identified the Murrah Federal Building as a possible target. Kerry Noble stated, "Richard Wayne Schnell wanted him to go with him to case out the place."

They mentioned it had minimum security, it was in the heartland and that no one would expect it. Schnell supposedly wanted to fill a vehicle with explosives. The group believes in divine intervention and while the person building the bomb dies when the bomb is accidentally detonated, the group sees this as it was not suppose to be.

The group lays low and approximately six months later Richard Schnell is stopped in a routine traffic stop. He shoots and kills a State Trooper. When authorities arrive they find a large store of illegal weapons in his vehicle. Richard Schnell was eventually tracked down in Oklahoma and arrested. He was tried and sentenced to death.

In the 1980's the government conducted operation Clean Sweep a Federal offensive against far right groups across the country. On April 18, 1985, a day recognized as Patriots Day by the far right, federal agents surround the CSA compound to indict the leaders on federal charges of manufacturing and possessing illegal firearms. When a standoff ensues, the government contacts a gentleman by the name of Robert Millar, who is known to have alliances with the CSA, and presides over his own religious compound, identified as Elohim city located in Oklahoma.

Robert Millar stated, "They asked me if I would be interested in preventing bloodshed, and I said of course, so they said all the men there were prepared to resist and to die. The leader said they don't trust anybody but Robert Millar that's me that's my name. So they flew me up there it was sort of a no man's land." On the third day Robert Millar persuades the CSA to surrender.

When the agents go into the compound they are astonished by what they find. They describe it as the largest confiscation of weapons and explosives in the history. They continue Operation Clean Sweep arresting more leaders of right wing organizations around the country charging them with robberies, counterfeiting, assassinations, bombings, and mass shootings.

Kerry Nobel's turned State's evidence along with other members of the CSA against Richard Wayne Schnell's 1983 plot to blowing up the Alfred P. Murrah Federal Building. The Jury fails to convict them despite the testimonies given. After seven weeks they are all cleared of all charges.

Timothy McVeigh a young man dealing with the divorce of his parents, was known as a loner and not athletic. In school he became obsessed with the Turner Diaries, the novel depicts the United States being thrust in to a race war, after a White supremacist uses a truck to blow up a federal building. In May of 1988 he enlists in the military. From here he begins distributing the Turner Diaries. Timothy McVeigh was committed to the book and its beliefs. He joined the KKK (Klu Klux Klan) a secret organization of white protestant Americans while he was in the Army where he met Terry Nichols, who was in his unit as well. In basic training he met and became friends with Michael Fortier a young anti American from Arizona. Timothy was awarded the Bronze Star after Iraq for meritorious service, he returns disillusioned. He opted out of the military returning to Pendleton, New York, where he gets employed by Burns security. In 1992 the Ruby Ridge incident sparked a fire in him. He left Burns security and for two years had no permanent address.

He traveled staying in mostly the southern states. In 1993 Waco, Texas, catches his attention when another event occurs. ATF agents raid the Branch Davidian compound creating the longest siege between civilians and the government in US history. Newly appointed Attorney General, Janet Reno, orders on April 19, 1993, which happens to be Patriots Day, a final assault on the compound leaving sixty nine men, women, and children dead.

Timothy McVeigh arrived to observe the incident and to hand out literature. He also used the alias Tim Tuttle to hide his true identity. We have covered some of the main characters, but is there more to this story of the Oklahoma Bombing?

Right from the start the Oklahoma City Police Department informed us to be on the lookout for two middle easterner suspects wearing blue jogging suits. Shortly before the bombing they were seen running from the Federal building getting into a brown pickup truck and driving away from the scene of the crime. It was soon determined that a truck bomb had exploded right outside the Alfred P. Murrah Federal Building. They were able to collect the vehicle identification number that was stamped on the twisted axel, which identified the vehicle as a Rider rental truck.

Sixty miles North of Oklahoma City Timothy McVeigh was pulled over for speeding without a license plate. It was the first time Timothy McVeigh had ever been arrested. The alert on the two middle Easterners had been rescinded within hours of the alert.

Terry Nichols after hearing the news that he was wanted for questioning in regards to the bombing, turned himself in to the Herrington, Kansas Police Department. Within twenty four hours from the attack the FBI had received a tip from a co-worker about Timothy McVeigh, from Buffalo, New York, who stated McVeigh had disposed militant government views and McVeigh was very angry at the siege that took place at the Branch Davidian, just outside Waco Texas. That event ended exactly to the day two years before the Oklahoma City Bombing.

Questions started to emerge, only adding more doubt and suspicion to an already traumatic event. From who the perpetrators were and why it happened. The ATF who had launched a raid on the Branch Davidians, had their Oklahoma office inside the Alfred P. Murrah Federal Building. The ATF were supposedly the target of the attack, yet no agents were killed or even injured. The agents were all tipped not to come to work that morning, by their pagers. When was the last time they had been tipped not to show up for work, and what was the reason?

The ATF gave several different stories explaining their agents absences, from two agents being inside the building and were seen as heroes. One agent Luke Franey, claims he was knocked unconscious during the blast and ended up crawling on the outside ledge of his office escaping, he used his martial arts skills to break through walls and injured his hand. Another agent claimed he was in the building in an elevator during the bombing. After freefalling for five floors, he broke out and rescued several people.

Oscar Johnson, an elevator mechanic stated, "None of the elevators suffered a free fall condition due to none of the governor over speeds were tripped." His crew was there before the fire department arrived. During the Grand Jury hearing the one agent stated he was in the elevator. Oscar Johnson stated they had checked all elevators and they were all still locked from the top that there was no one inside them. That no one could have gotten out of the elevators without assistance.

Jane Graham worked in the building over ten years and was Vice President of the Federal employees Union. She was familiar with most the people that worked there. Jane noted that she had seen two suspicious persons standing in front by the double doors wearing ATF jackets, they were talking to a third gentleman dressed in a business suit. She mentioned that when the ATF go up there to their office they are never identifiable.

An ambulance driver, Tiffany Bible confirmed that the agents were not in the office and that they may have been aware of a threat that day. She stated on her affidavit that she had spoken to an ATF agent asking if there was any of them in the building, and the agent said no, there was no one in the building. The agent also stated the Murrah building was blown up due to Waco. She also stated she saw at least eight ATF agents outside the building in clean Black jumpsuits with in twenty minutes of the incident.

The US Marshall service warned federal agencies of a possible Islamic fundamentalist attack. This was reported in the New Jersey Star Ledge on March 15, 1995.

Carol Howe was placed by the ATF as an informant into a white separatist community known as Elohim city. Another agent had stated that Andy Strassmeir had made threats to blow up federal buildings, this was before the Oklahoma City bombing, and that they actually drove to Oklahoma City to scout targets.

A US Representative of Oklahoma, Ernest Istook was said to have had prior knowledge, as he was talking with Sherriff Deputy David Kochendorfer. The Deputy stated Ernest Istook said, "Yea we knew this was going to happen."

Sheriff Deputy Don Hammonds stated he noticed a women taking pictures, she identified herself as an attorney and she was with Ernest Istook. She made a comment that they were aware of a bomb threat since April 9th, ten days before the bombing. Ernest Istook has denied the evidence under oath, but has also refused to do a polygraph test as well.

Witnesses say that the bomb squad was conducting a search at the court house across the street from the Murrah building two hours before the attack. Others had seen the bomb disposal unit parked outside the court house that morning. The Sherriff Department denies this claim.

The Oklahoma City bombing made news on the television episode 20/20 approximately eighteen months later. Questions were being asked and more information was being brought out to the public.

Authorities then claimed that the truck was being used by a Deputy to run errands. 20/20 presented a document showing, someone had called the Department of Justice twenty four minutes prior to the bombing. The caller said, "The federal building in Oklahoma City has just been bombed." This was before the bomb had gone off and no action apparently was taken. 20/20 was working on a full segment about prior knowledge, but the Justice Department supposedly intervened. Feds came in and told them they could not do the episode on prior knowledge.

Could this be why we look at the media not as watch dogs that are there to inform us of any wrong doing, but as merely pawns, or actors being told what to say and rehearsing their parts and, or scripts?

Governor Frank Keating's brother, Mark had been writing a novel about a bombing in Oklahoma City before the bombing occurred and the characters name was Thomas McVeigh.

Don Browning, an officer with the Oklahoma City Police Department stated that their special unit with horses and county reserve officers were activated to help with crowd control that morning before the bombing occurred. He stated that it was very rare that they worked the downtown area.

The question of whether Timothy McVeigh worked alone or with someone remains a topic of interest, as the FBI and DOJ (Department of Justice) first released two sketches of the subjects that parked the truck in front of the Murrah building, to then focusing only on McVeigh.

The question then becomes who was the other subject, and what happened to him? Rodney Johnson stated, "I know for a fact Timothy McVeigh was with another individual on the morning of April 19th, right before the bombing."

State Representative Charles Key stated, "they chose to not pursue other individuals." These individuals were unknown, not Terry Nichols, or Michael Fortier.

A covenant store clerk stated he, or she had witnessed Timothy McVeigh getting gas in a rental truck two days earlier.

In the USA Today news paper they had printed an article titled, FBI Manhunt. Stating the following, "The men suspected of renting the truck used to carry the bomb are called "armed and dangerous."

John Doe #1 White medium build, 5'9 to 5'10, weighing 175 to 180 pounds, brown hair, he has a tattoo visible beneath T-shirt sleeve on left arm, possible smoker.

John Doe #2 White medium build, 5'9 or 5'11, weighing 180 to 185 pounds, light brown crew cut, right handed call with information to 1-800-905-1514.

To me that seems like some very detailed information about two subjects that were considered armed and dangerous. So did they find information on who these people were? Were the eye witnesses later seen as incorrect on their descriptions?

Were these people that were never meant to be found? Why did it get published in the USA Today news paper and who gave the newspaper the information?

The government stated McVeigh never scouted inside the Murrah building, a secret service member stated she had seen him inside the building along with a second suspect.

The official report is that Timothy McVeigh rented the truck alone on April 17, 1995, two days before the bombing. McVeigh and Terry Nichols supposedly constructed the bomb on April 18th, but many witnesses state the Ryder truck was seen at Geary Lake in Kansas several days before that.

Now I know you have to be thinking the same thing I am, there are hundreds of Ryder trucks out there how do we know this is the one. James Sergeant stated he had seen the truck out there at the lake and he mentioned he was sitting home one day when his wife got home told him that she had been stopped up here at Geary Lake, in reference to the Oklahoma City Bombing and the making of the bomb here at Geary Lake with a Ryder truck. His wife had told the ATF and FBI what her husband had seen. He said before he knew it his house was swarming with agents.

Witnesses state that Timothy McVeigh was seen staying at the Dreamland motel, just outside Fort Riley Kansas with the Ryder truck, days before and another person was with him.

There are accusations that more than one Ryder truck was involved and more people than the government is letting on.

Craig Roberts, a police officer in Tulsa Oklahoma for twenty seven years stated in 1995 when the bombing occurred that he was requested by the FBI office and chief of police, to assist in any way he could. He worked with some other law enforcement, one officer was one of the first on scene and he saw the greatest damage came in the pit, which was in the back of the building and went down two or three floors. That information never came out in the news and was not considered part of the investigation. Craig Robert stated if it didn't fit what the DOJ and Janet Reno wanted it to fit it was discarded.

In the bombing there were eight people who had left legs amputated, yet there were nine legs one was unidentified meaning there was someone who was missing? Did anyone ever identify who the leg belonged to or was there still an unknown victim waiting to be discovered? Was this person some accidental victim, or purposely targeted? Could it belong to one of the bombers? How is it we do not have an answer yet?

T.K. Marshall, Pathologist for Northern Ireland stated, "In all the years in Ireland, we identified every innocent person that was killed. There was never an unknown Victim."

We have cameras, witnesses, DNA, special agents trained in recovery of evidence, so what is our excuse for not knowing? I am sure we are not incompetent?

An FBI agent admitted that the 1,034 fingerprints collected during the investigation under oath were not run through the National Fingerprint Data Base. Was this done just to go through the motions, making everyone think a big investigation was being done? Why else would you collect them if you had no intention of following through? Was this to deceive us all?

They focus on the Ryder being the bomb yet there were two other bombs that they had reported on, that had not yet detonated. Looking at this were these bombs all suppose to go off at the same time? Were they set to trigger the next bomb? Were there multiple people each having the responsibility of their own bomb? Could the truck bomb went off earlier than it was planned to killing the other bomber, catching him off guard, making that leg that was unidentified his?

The Media again was presenting the bombing differently than it had the day prior, with the exception to KFOR-TV who continued with the news it had covered earlier. The New York Times broadcasting company purchased the company a year after the bombing and fired the programming director, the lead journalist on the bombing, Jayna Davis, who was let go, and all reporting's contradicting the government then vanished as well.

A law enforcement officer was told by an FBI agent, the kind of comments you make, people like you often end up dead. Is this not a threat at the highest level possible? Was this agent warning him in good faith to be silent, or was he intimidating him? Either way the agent is aware of some sort of conspiracy. Remember conspiracy is to conspire between two people, or more.

One of the Grand Jurors stated they were not given the tapes that showed who got out of the vehicles and that all the tapes were sealed preventing them from seeing all the evidence. At what point does the government itself become liable for impeding an investigation?

The Oklahoma City bombing was moved to Colorado and lasted only three weeks, they compared it to the OJ Simpson trial that lasted near nine months. Why was this such a short trial? Why was it moved out of Oklahoma? Was justice really served that day or is this just another façade created by the elite to conceal a more dubious plan?

Just before his death the FBI announced they had withheld thousands of pages of documents that could have swayed, or influenced this trial. Is this again the federal government preventing a person from a fair and impartial trial. Was he then not found guilty before having all the evidence heard? Where was his presumed innocent until proven guilty option at? If he were guilty and all the evidence was presented he would have been then honorably found guilty, but instead we may never know the truth, as a shadow of truth is always just outside of reach.

There was Officer Yeakey, who was brutally murdered beaten and shot. He just happened to be one of the officers that arrived first on scene that day when the Murrah building blew up. He supposedly made the statement that he had to run an errand and would be back after he shook the Feds. He never made it home, he was found later dead.

The question is who and why, is this all related, or just a coincidence? They classified his death as a suicide, yet they state there were no powder burns. So if it is a suicide how can they claim this when the evidence doesn't show this, as they point out all the physical abuse he sustained, plus the bloody knife that was found in the locked vehicle, along with the bullet wound from a small caliber weapon?

They mentioned the Ryder truck was packed with 1,200 pounds of ammonia nitrate then it was changed into 4,800 pounds and again into 7,000 pounds of fertilizer and nitro methane. Were these changes being made because they were collecting more information and evidence, or was it being changed to fit the narrative?

They talk about the truck creating an air blast that would release its energy simultaneously in every direction. They mentioned if the truck is in front of something bigger than it can take out it would create a semi circle.

Craig Roberts, who is a police officer stated he had worked on a bomb squad and that the damage done didn't match the trucks capability.

They showed all the debris out in the street after the bombing that blew in to the blast rather than away from the blast. If it looks like another bomb exploded it probably did. There is a lot more out there if you're willing to search for the facts.

If you are ready, we will move on to our next story, as Deception, shadows of truth continues.

RUBY RIDGE

Ruby Ridge, located in Northern Idaho became one of the deadliest confrontations in Idaho's history, as Federal agents swarmed in to take out a fugitive that was living on the mountain with his family.

Randy Weaver was living on the mountain with his wife Vicky, their children Rachel, Sam, and Sarah, along with their friend Kevin Harris. Randy Weaver and his wife Vicky were married in Fort Dodge, Iowa in 1971. In 1983 they packed up and headed out West to the mountains of Idaho, here he was going to raise his family and live a free life that he wanted to share with his family.

In 1992 a siege took place leaving his son Sam, his wife Vicky, and a US Marshall Deputy William Francis Degan all dead. The siege became a stand for justice and constitutional rights, when law enforcement came in with military might and limited rules of engagement.

The Arian headquarters were just seventy miles from Randy's home. The FBI and ATF, along with other local law enforcement agencies were focusing on these groups due to terrorist activities in the North. They had just taken out a radical group known as the Order, which had bombed banks, hijacked armored cars, as well as murdered a Jewish talk show host. Randy Weaver was approached by a Secret Federal Informant posing as a biker at one of these rallies called the World Congress, it's a gathering of White separatists and people with certain types of philosophy.

The informant known as Gus Magesono becomes friends with an attendee known as Randy Weaver. Gus slowly works on gaining Randy's trust and offers him $700.00 for two sawed off shotguns. In October 1989 he saws the barrels off and sells the guns to Gus. Not long after Randy finds out that Gus is a snitch and breaks ties with him.

The ATF who were using Magesono now were without an informant. They look to replace him with Randy Weaver. Randy stated the Agency said they would bring Federal firearm charges against him if he did not cooperate.

Randy Weaver stated, "I am not going to join your team and become an informant. If I would have joined their team and became a snitch for them than none of this would of happened."

ATF Agents posing as tourist with an overheated vehicle waited for Randy and Vicky to approach and when he did they told him to "freeze Federal Agents."

One year later after selling the guns Randy is arrested, during his arraignment he is allowed to sign over his property as bond. The magistrate tells him if he is found guilty his property will be taken away.

Randy's paranoia of the government makes him feel his only option is to stay on the mountain. Here Randy can chose his own destiny rather than by a court he does not fully trust.

Rachel stated it was their whole family's decision, that they wanted their whole family to stay together on the mountain, rather than have her dad go to jail for gun violations.

Randy stated he heard on the radio that he was identified as a White supremacist that didn't show up for court and the US Marshalls will get their man.

Once he missed his court hearing he then became a Federal fugitive and his case was turned over to the US Marshalls.

Allen Jeppeson was a friend that asked Randy Weaver if he sawed the barrels off the shotguns. Randy told him no, that he did not do that. Allen also stated he felt Randy was being picked on due to his political views and if it could happen to Randy it could happen to him as well.

In April of 1991 the Marshalls send the letters Vicky had written along with the case file to a Psychologist, for a psychological profile.

They had mistaken the Weavers as the Randall's, as they paint a picture of a paranoid family lead by a fierce matriarch who are all willing to fight to their death.

As the months pass the Weavers remain held up on the mountain top and the Marshalls remain hesitant to approach fearing an altercation, they communicate through friends. In October of 1991 Vicky gives birth to their fourth child, a baby girl in a shed.

With winter on the way the Weavers prepare for the long months ahead, while the US Marshalls leave the Weavers alone with other cases taking priority. On March 8, 1992 one year later a local newspaper runs an article about a wanted fugitive snubbing his nose at authorities of the Federal Government. Within days this gets national media and Randy Weaver is seen as a thorn in the side of the US. Marshalls.

Three weeks after the news article they hold a meeting at the US Marshalls headquarters. Where they focus on the Weavers setting up surveillance and apprehension, calling it Operation Northern Exposure. During the next five months the US Marshalls record over one hundred hours of surveillance footage from solar powered cameras strategically placed throughout the area. The family is seen as usually always armed and ready for any confrontation. They also see a man they recognize as Kevin Harris who grew up with them as a teenager.

The media is fixed on the Weavers and Randy is seen as a folk hero and his cabin then is seen as a fortress, which it was not.

In the early hours of August 21,1992, six US Marshalls fully armed and with night observation gear approach to gather more intelligence for the final phase. After eight hours the team turns to head down the mountain with what information they had gathered, but Randy Weaver's dog started barking alerting him. He thought it might be a bear or a mountain lion. Randy headed down there with Sam and Kevin behind him. Randy stated the dog took off barking and Randy headed down the logging road. He told Sam and Kevin he would meet them down at the Y. The other two headed after the dog through the woods. Sam and Kevin were both armed anticipating a wild animal.

Randy stated an agent dressed in full cameo with a weapon, jumped out and said "freeze Weaver." He then turned and said "screw you and turned went running back up the mountain yelling get on boys, get on boys it's an ambush."

The boys didn't hear Randy and continued chasing the dog. Then Randy heard a bang, as well as a yap from his dog. He yelled, "they shot the dog, they shot the dog." Through the chaos Sam is struck and killed along with one US Marshall.

Two of the Us Marshalls that were not involved in the gun fight and were unfamiliar with the area, run through the woods for nearly an hour where they get to a neighbors house and make a call to 911.

The 911 call is important to get a good perspective of what was going through the minds of the officers at the time.

The officer states to the 911 operator the following, "I got one officer dead. I got three pinned down. I need help quick. We had an incident with Randall Weaver. I want State Police. I want all the help I can get. I've got to go back in for more officers that are trapped."

We find out that no officers were trapped and the US Marshalls were not aware of the losses on the Weaver's side.

Kevin returned to the cabin and advised Randy that his fourteen year old son, Sam was killed in a fire fight. He was shot once in the arm and once in the back. Randy stated he lost it. He said no one yelled at them or shot anymore, so he figured they had all split. Randy, Vicky, and Kevin go to retrieve Sam's body bringing it back up to the cabin. They place him in the cabin where his baby sister was born months before.

The local law enforcement evacuates the neighbors and closes off the entire mountain. On August 21, 1992 The FBI for the first time hears of Randy Weaver and Ruby Ridge as Gene Glenn, FBI Special Agent in charge stated they were advised there was a shooting at Ruby Ridge and that a US Marshall had been killed, and other Marshalls were pinned down. He stated they had two objectives going up there, number one the rescuing of the US Marshalls, and number two, the arresting of Randy Weaver.

They activate the HRT (Hostage Rescue Team) This is an elite unit of the FBI's, known as possibly the most elite snipers and assaulters in the world.

Dick Rodgers, the head of the HRT consults with FBI Director Larry Potts on the way to Idaho, they agree that the intelligence that they were receiving on the Weaver family warranted extreme measures. They draft special rules of engagement that give the agents more freedom than what they give on their standard policies.

They mention that the shooting had subsided and that the Marshalls were taken back down the mountain by the State Police.

Fred Lanceley, Head Negotiator FBI commented that he had been in over 300 negotiations before but he had a bad feeling about this one.

On Day two, near twenty four hours after the shooting, law enforcement from all over start to gather to a central location on the mountain top. A briefing ensues with FBI negotiators, HRT tactical team, and Gene Glenn the On Scene Commander. The presence of the FBI's Light Armored vehicle Carrier, created an intimidating presence that brought the anger out of those that were observing, both neighbors and friends, along with anti government groups.

Dick Rodgers told everyone that any adult male with a gun was a target. It was stated in the rules of engagement that any adult male is observed with a weapon, deadly force can and should be employed.

Snipers are deployed around the area to make a perimeter, while the FBI prepare to approach the cabin.

Randy stated that the dogs started barking and he figured there was somebody out there that wanted to talk to them, So he went outside with his sixteen year old daughter Sarah, and Kevin Harris to see if anyone was outside. After he gets no response he heads over to the guest shed where Sam's body was placed the day before.

As he reaches up to unsecure the latch, he gets shot in the shoulder. Vicky hears the shot and goes to the front door and yells for Randy and the others to get back inside. Sarah and Kevin ran following Randy as Vicky held the door for them, as she held on to their youngest in her arms. Suddenly a shot rings out as a bullet goes through Vicky's head killing her, as it then hits Kevin in the arm and stop just short of his heart.

The reality was sinking in as three laid dead and two were wounded. Randy stated on video that he didn't even care anymore that he just wanted to take a few with him. This would be the mind set of any normal person after you lose your son and see your wife killed right before you, along with being shot and in pain and wondering where that next shot was going to come from.

Dick Rodgers, the head of the HRT gave him an ultimatum to either come out or we are going to crush your buildings. If you remember they brought in the FBI's Light Armored vehicle Carrier, an extremely intimidating piece of machinery if you are on the other side of it. If Randy didn't feel backed in a corner before I am sure he did then. Randy did not respond back. Both sides were standing firm and the spectators were growing increasingly agitated with the excessive force of the Federal agents, who they seen as coming in taking over.

On day three reporters broadcast over the television that all Randy Weaver wants is to be left alone as more law enforcement and helicopters are continuing to arrive, as the standoff becomes unavoidable.

The FBI Head Negotiator, Fred Lanceley stated even he thought all this was extreme as he stated we need all this for one man his wife and children? They brought in earth moving equipment to widen the road and build a bridge so they could get larger trucks up there to their location.

They mentioned how the area turned into more of a community as some guys were getting off work others were just starting. They showed guys playing horseshoes as they relaxed on their off time.

Don Kusulas, FBI swat team member, was one who spoke out against the rules of engagement. The negotiators thought this was an easy solution, to just sit and wait Weaver out. They used their heavy equipment to clear out the area around the cabin. They stopped before they hit the shed, as one agent jumped out checking the shed only to find Sam's lifeless body. It sends a shockwave through the agency, as no one knew of any of the Weavers losses.

On day four they let the public know of Randy's son Sam who had died in the shoot out. The residents were not taking the news well as the friends and family, neighbors and outside protestors became more vocal. What suddenly seemed like a strategic plan now looked more like an out of control abuse of authority by the government.

On day five the FBI investigate the area of where the shootout took place, what they found was that it appeared the information they had received from the US Marshalls may have been greatly exaggerated. The FBI did not find the amount of rounds that would show a shoot out that would create a twelve hour battle.

On day six in Quincy Massachusetts, a funeral is held for Deputy William Degan who was killed in the shootout. His body was carried by United States Marines dressed in their dress blues. It was a sad day for both sides of the battlefield.

Randy and Kevin dictate a note to Sarah in case they do not make it off the mountain alive, while more people continue to gather down below.

On day seven a gentleman by the name of Bo Gritz arrives, he is a retired colonel, a green beret commander. He was there in hopes of talking to Weaver. When Weaver found out he was there he requested to speak to Bo, who was also a right wing icon. On day eight they allowed Bo Gritz to head up the mountain to talk to Randy.

Bo was able to accomplish more in one evening than the rest were able to in the seven days. Randy was finally able to tell Bo that Vicky had been killed and that him and Kevin were both shot as well. No one knew of this. When the friends and neighbors heard about Vicky's death it fueled the flames once again as emotions ran high. The whole time the FBI thought Vicky was just another active participant of this defiant stand.

Day nine came and Bo went to talk with Randy once again. Randy explains what happened and brings to Bo's attention about the robot they used that dropped off the phone, it had a 12 gauge shotgun mounted on it pointed at the door. The FBI state that was an oversight.

Bo approached Jackie Brown a family friend asking her if she would go up with him. She said it happened before she knew it She was allowed to take a few supplies up there with Bo. The Weavers let her in when she got up there. Jackie even stated that if the Weavers or anyone would have stuck their heads out they would had been shot, that was her feelings of the situation.

On day ten Bo heads up there with one objective and that was to get Kevin Harris out, his wounds were becoming infected and he needed immediate medical treatment. Bo stated to Randy, "If I have anything to do with this, if I can testify before the jury, if I were on the jury, you would fry if you let that boy die in here." Kevin surrenders at 1:47 pm and he is treated at a medical tent before being rushed out on helicopter, to a Washington hospital.

Bo and Jackie return to get Vicky's body. Bo carried her body back down the mountain and Jackie asked for water to clean up the blood that was inside. The FBI brought her two buckets of water. Her intentions I'm sure were to clean up the area to be more presentable, but evidence was lost that way due to being disturbed.

On day eleven Bo went up to let Randy know his time was up he had to go now or they were going to come in and take them out. Randy agreed, the siege was over.

Eleven days later with three dead, two others wounded the siege was finally over. This was a sad story, one that many I am sure would like to forget. Was this a story of conspiracy, deception, or fraud? I'm not so sure about conspiracy, but appears to have some deception in it as you look at how the US Marshalls portrayed the Weavers and how they over exaggerated the shootout on the mountain. It could be looked at as just another example of the government using excessive force through mass build up of specialized forces for the purpose of intimidation and or to complete the job at any cost.

We have to look at this story and ask could this story have inspired others on the Oklahoma bombing, to retaliate on the government? Was Waco seen as the straw that broke the camel's back? Are these stories all entwined with one another?

Bo Gritz was a hero who was able to come into a crisis situation and mediate for both sides, bringing this to a resolve that all wanted and needed.

Kevin Harris and Randy Weaver were charged with murder and conspiracy. After a three month trial Kevin was found not guilty on all charges and released. Randy was found not guilty of all but the failure to appear charge. He serves an additional six months in jail. The FBI did admit to covering up facts during the trial.

The Weavers filed a civil suit against the federal government and it was settled out of court. There is no mountain to big and no man so small, let that say it all.

Ruby Ridge

Let not this lesson be forgotten. As much as no man
is above the law, neither is an agency.

BOSTON BOMBING

On April 15, 2013 people had gathered both as spectators, as well as participants in an event known as the Boston Marathon. It was one of the prestigious of all marathons. People from all over the world came to take part in this event, but on this day it was not those that made it to the finish line that were going to be remembered. Instead those that died or were injured as innocent bystanders, along with those that would later be accused of perpetuating this whole ordeal.

At 2:49 pm EDT an explosion occurs near the finish line, twelve seconds later 210 yards further away a second explosion goes off. As two puffs of white smoke clouds and confuses those around the area.

Once again a beautiful day has been tarnished by those we call terrorists, those who are willing to kill others for a cause whether or not innocent lives are taken or not.

War has hit the streets of Boston, Massachusetts

America's news commentators are quick to report on the scene, as Americans listen for clarity of what happened.

This event was thought to be terrorist organized, catching us all off guard. Now years later this story too makes it in the pages of Deception, with questions of conspiracy, and fraud. Follow us as we look at this event closer.

The Federal Bureau of Investigation took over the investigation and three days later on April 18, 2013 they released the photos of Dzhokhar Tsarnaev and Tamerlan Tsarnaev publically. They are Chechen brothers. Shortly after the release of the photos, the subjects kill an MIT police officer, and hijack a civilian SUV. They ensue in a gun battle between themselves and the police in Watertown, Massachusetts.

Tamerlan Tsarnaev was shot several times in the gun battle, along with being rundown by the same vehicle they used to escape and evade with by his own brother. Tamerlan Tsarnaev was pronounced dead at the scene.

Thousands of law enforcement personnel swarmed the area of Watertown, covering a twenty block radius. Businesses, local institutions, along with public transportation were all shut down temporarily on a very large scale. People were asked to stay inside and to lock their doors.

Eventually Dzhokhar Tsarnaev was located behind a house in a boat unsure if armed or not he was shot and arrested then treated at a hospital.

CNN reports on the Boston Marathon bombing as they mention both Chechen brothers, Dzhokhar Tsarnaev and Tamerlan Tsarnaev were preparing across the Charles river with their own agenda. They had been viewing the magazine called Inspire which was created by Al-Qaida the terror group in the Arabian Peninsula. They look at a recipe on making a bomb in your mother's kitchen.

They talk about using pressure cookers and everyday items referring to nails for shrapnel. They were reported to have gone to the Home Depot in Cambridge to buy a soldering gun, fireworks that they used the gunpowder out of the fireworks, along with BBs to be placed in their homemade bomb.

As CNN covers the story they point out the location of the two brothers. You can see on the one video that the younger brother, Dzhokhar puts a phone to his ear as seconds later an explosion goes off as everyone looks towards the blast and he turns and heads the other way and again seconds later the next bomb goes off right in the same area that the younger brother was just standing. You can see in the video that Dzhokhar leaves the area quickly and then you see him twenty four minutes later in a store buying milk as though nothing has happened. He clearly knows what has happened, as he is seen on the tape looking towards the first explosion.

In his defense though other people were in there shopping as well. The difference is that if he initiated the explosions he appears to be cold and heartless. In the video you can also see clearly that he is without his backpack that he had twenty four minutes earlier.

Dzhokhar's friends identified him as normal. Dzhokhar arrived in 2002 speaking very little English at the age of eight years old. He grew up and became a wrestling captain on his Cambridge wrestling team. He was liked by many.

His brother Tamerlan Tsarnaev, was seven years older than him and was having a harder time adjusting to American culture. Unlike Dzhokhar who was well liked and had many friends Tamerlan had none. Their sisters too were failing with marriages and their parents with earning a living. Tamerlan found a sense of belonging in radical Islam. Him and his mother received a visit from the FBI who interviewed them on concerns of radicalism, but nothing came of it due to lack of evidence.

Tamerlan heads to Dagestan next to Chechnya. Dagestan is torn by ethnic violence and extremism. It is during this visit that something happens that connects with Tamerlan and he passes information and idealism back to his brother, Dzhokhar. When Tamerlan returned six months later he is noticed as more radical and him and his brother listen to radical Islamist messages.

As the forensic teams sift through the crime scene area looking for evidence, they find parts of the pressure cookers, parts of the back pack and a twisted fuse. They also go over and over the videos looking at things that stands out. One of those items was none other than Dzhokhar who is seen on the video during the bombing not flinching and moving away in the opposite direction very clearly. They point out that Dzhokhar text a friend telling him if he wants he can take what's there, referring to his property.

The brothers appear to have no plan thought out, making you wonder on that note by itself if they had concocted this on their own or if they had taken direction from someone else.

On the video you see where the brothers, or the subjects approach the officers vehicle and then are seen running from the vehicle in the same direction that they came from. Tamerlan and his brother hijack an SUV telling the driver they were the ones that did the Boston Marathon Bombing, and that they shot a police officer.

The driver escapes from his own vehicle when they pulled into get gas. The driver runs into another convenience store and asks them to call 911, stating that he was hijacked by the guys that did the Boston bombing. Police respond and use the GPS to track the vehicle to Watertown where the shootout took place.

The shootout was intense as Tamerlan runs out of ammunition and WAs tackled by officers. His brother Dzhokhar sees this and heads the vehicle towards the officers that were wrestling with his brothers as the police are being warned to get out of the way. Dzhokhar continues driving towards them, but misses the officers and runs his brother over instead killing him.

Dzhokhar escapes temporarily and the town is put on lockdown. He is eventually found in a boat in one of the residents back yard. He was shot and arrested, then treated medically. In the boat Dzhokhar left a note that he had written reported by CNN it said, " The U.S. Government is killing our innocent civilians... I can't stand to see such evil go unpunished."

He wrote as well the following saying, "We Muslims are one body, you hurt one you hurt us all." He also stated, "I'm jealous of my brother... I do not mourn because his soul is very much alive." Dzhokhar was charged with thirty federal counts, including conspiring to use a weapon of mass destruction. Dzhokhar pleads not guilty. In the end he is found guilty of all the charges.

In another video you can see someone had videoed the bombing on their supposed cell phone. On the video when they slow it down you do not see any blood. What you do see is a woman that is wearing red and during the crisis is not bloody in two separate pictures shown later you see her in a wheel chair with an injured left hand and face, to me looks very suspicious.

In the one video you can see a hand on a leg as he is directing the person in the wheel chair by jerking the leg in the intended direction. If this were real then the person who is handling the leg, I would say is no professional. They point out the reason for shaking the leg was to make sure it was securely attached for the wheel chair ride in front of the cameras.

There is the controversy with Jeff Bauman's left leg being amputated long before the bombing as they show two pictures of his left leg with a bulge, along with another picture that shows his leg with no bruising or irritation, but instead what looks like a healthy healed leg. On the very same video they point out the tattoos on his arms saying they could have been erased. That seems like a lot of thinking for this event but all should be looked at. They want you to focus on the length of the stubs, which are longer in some pictures and shorter in others.

They point out on the video his left thigh is too long, relative to his arm. They point out his left leg if they add a foot to it, which they do using photo ops on the video. They say if his left leg is too long his right leg is even longer. They point at his right knee cap protruding out in a certain position.

They do bring up the question why does he look so calm and not in shock, which can be argued either way. But he does look well poised and not in any pain like I would think one would be in after losing a leg, or two.

There is also the Marathon hero who wore a cowboy hat, his name was Carlos Arredondo. At the beginning of the video you see Carlos with another gentleman holding up a sign that says, (Latinos remaking America). They then mention that Carlos had come from Costa Rica across Arizona in 1980 and obtained his green card by testifying against the people he paid to bring him here. They mention his ex-wife is Melida Arredondo, who is a peace activist. While it is true America is made up of diversity it does seem like activists, as well as lobbyists are uniquely woven together whether by accident or on purpose in these chaotic crisis.

Carlos was identified as a hero who had jumped and cleared fences along with helping rescue and save Jeff Bauman, who had lost both limbs as they mention he had his arteries severed in his legs. They point out if both arteries are cut then it increases the severity of the injury to include death by bleeding out. On the video you would expect to find Carlos attending to Jeff who needs immediate attention, but we do not see that.

What we see is a man that tries to appear to be helping while he clinches hold of the American flag. It makes me wonder if he is holding the flag so we know what team he is on. What would make a person focus so much on the flag when there are those that need our help? It is possible he sees himself helping a cause rather than a person. In the video you do see him handed something that he sticks in his pocket from someone in a yellow jacket. He does take the time to look at it as he puts it in his pocket which is later identified as a bloody flag. Carlos mentions as he is interviewed that he dropped the flag, which we do not see on video at any time. Though again if he did drop the flag why not continue on helping Americans in dire straits?

Carlos states that he picked up Jeff and put him in the wheelchair. This too would seem odd when there are people all over that could help assist him, and would if this was real. Jeff too stated that Carlos was the one that picked him up off the ground. What they forget to mention is the other people that were caught on camera lifting Jeff up into a wheelchair. It is possible Jeff was in shock at that moment. Carlos had tunnel vision, focusing only on what he thought was his mission to get Jeff in the wheelchair. There were two other people besides himself that took him by wheelchair out of the crisis area, or crime scene, which ever you prefer to call it.

He mentions he is part of Red Cross and is somewhat trained in disasters, yet the word tourniquet he had to have said to him by his ex-wife. I know we all have forgotten words before, so yes it is possible. I am trying to be fair to both sides of the conspiracies.

On the video he says he is a member of the Red Cross as he holds up a badge. Could this be one of those badges we heard about in the Sandy Hook story? In the video you see him bend down and attach what appears to be a new badge to his chain as he struggles getting it over his cowboy hat. He is seen with two different badges, why?

If you listened to enough of the witnesses that were there they will tell you they saw FBI agents and bomb sniffing dogs early on. They will tell you the FBI were conducting a bomb exercise there at the same time. Is this just a coincidence or was it part of the exercise?

They show Carlos phone, where he showed a picture of Jeff laying in agony. Why would you be focused on taking pictures if not for a cause, or some sadistic purpose of pleasure, or monetary gains?

On the Boston Hero or NOW FRAUD video you see areas where people are not standing or sitting, one minute, then you see them laying and positioned in a manner that looks staged.

Carlos mentioned that Jeff's shirt was on fire when it is clear it is not, was not, or will ever be, yet he sticks with this statement. There is also the changing of the cowboy hats where they show you two distinctly different hats one that says Costa Rica on it in the front while the other does not.

You may think does a hat really matter? Well it does if it is missing evidence such as blood. They show a picture of his hat during the April bombing and one month later. I guess it took them a month to alter the hat.

I guess the hat matters enough to put it on eBay and sell it for, a buy it now price of One Million Dollars. Just another perfect example of raising money from what is suppose to be a real crisis. I wonder how much he wants for the bloody flag?

His shirt is not without critiquing, as we see no blood on the sleeve till later in one interview, yet we have seen his sleeve in clear view as he is assisting Jeff in the wheelchair. You would think too, if he lifted Jeff as he said he did there would be more blood on his shirt. The truth is that he had help and the video substantiates that.

His pants too showed no blood on them during the interview and later in the video from Amy Goodman's he has blood all over them. It again makes me think of Sandy Hook as the hero becomes the Ponzi. Where so much attention is put on them it is hard to keep the facts straight and the scenes in order.

You see during the explosion the flags were just fine, but listening to Carlos Arredondo the flags were all gone, destroyed. The truth is the flags appeared to have not even been torn, shredded, punctured by any shrapnel. What are the odds of that being possible considering all the flags that were there in the bombs path?

Let's look at Carlos's history. On August 25, 2004 Carlos was outside his home in Hollywood, Florida when three marines arrived to give him the news his son Alexander had been killed in Iraq. He loses it and torches the van the marines arrived in setting himself on fire by mistake as well.

Two days after the van attack Carlos wakes up to two strangers by his bedside. He called them officers and stated this case was taken over by the FBI and Homeland Security. He admits he thought he was in trouble for targeting U.S. Government property. He mentioned everything was taken care of.

Carlos stated after his son died President Bush signed a security order, giving citizenship to parents of the sons and daughters that died in the Iraq War. He stated, "I received the first one granted to a parent, with the help of Senator Kennedy." Remember he is an illegal immigrant. He is not deported or sent to Guantanamo, he was not charged with destroying government property, or given a bill for his hospital stay. He did however receive a first class trip from Florida to Massachusetts for three, for his son's funeral. This is supposedly when all the press coverage began.

The media focuses on Carlos and Melida, and not his first wife Victoria who actually raised his children. They portray Melida as the grieving mother. It is possible that the media was just duped by a woman who tries to slide in and replace Victory who never seems to get mentioned. We know Melida as an activist, but the video points out opportunist as well. When Melida says they were responsible for their son's service, this is a perfect example of deception. You then have to ask why does all this matter unless you have an objective, or agenda. Who is it they are wanting to impress or influence? Maybe they are using all this to pay a debt back to someone with elite authority?

He who looks away from the obvious is just as blind

On a radio interview Carlos and Melida couldn't even agree on whether or not they had talked with the family of the guy they saved?

We are only humane but in my entire life I have never known anyone to allow a news media, or photographer in to take pictures of those grieving over their loved ones. I have to sound the alarm of skepticism on this issue. A respected Time Magazine that is political doing a story on this? Was it the loss of a Marine, or focused on an illegal who got a second chance?

Carlos has been paid with free travel, free publicity and notoriety he has been honored all over at games and has spoken at political conventions does he not standout as someone very special?

On this same video they point out how racism is used to separate this country, because a country divided can't come together to protect itself, which is what the elite want supposedly. To prove that statement they show a clip from none other than the famous Opera Winfrey who stated the following, "There are still generations of people, older people who are born and bred and marinated in that prejudice of racism and they just have to die."

Why do these people have to die? Should we not educate others on racism and know if we can educate the old the young will follow? I know this all seems to come out of nowhere, but it is the idea that the bombing at the Boston Marathon was fake as we have covered some interesting points that would be hard to dispute, along with the links that will show you with your own eyes.

On another video you see a picture of the victim Jeff Bauman, who is identified as Nick Vogt. I could be wrong on the last name, but he is a former U.S. Army officer who lost his legs in Kandahar, Afghanistan. He was with the 1st Stryker Brigade 25th infantry division in 2011. This is what they report on the video.

Let's look at this next picture and tell me what you see.

Another victim that has died twice, you would think with today's technology they would do makeup to at least mask the obvious. I am not sure if the crisis actors are getting better or worse, but Americans are waking up to the trickery. If this is true who can and will explain this? I would love to hear any reasonable explanation.

On this video they claim that former CIA agent, Robert David Steele has declared that the Sandy Hook and the Boston Marathon bombing were false flags, where a staged event is presented to influence a targeted audience.

Nicole Brannock Gross reportedly broke both her tibia and fibula on both her legs, while she sits calmly for twenty minutes waiting to be treated or showcased.

There is one CNN crisis actor that has been caught four times as GMN reports, she was caught at the actual Boston marathon bombing, then in Watertown, and also in Sandy Hook shooting. This was on a video called Crisis actor caught again 4th time. The last one was the NTSB train derailment.

You would think that they could find new actors, instead of using the very same ones. Some of this information came from the Pete Santilli Show. On another video they show once again a different girl that they say was at the Sandy Hook, Boston Marathon, and Aurora. They state the reason for crisis actors is to throw out a perception to say things without giving details. That tells me it is not about perception, but deception.

In one video Victoria McGrath is seen being carried by a first responder She was supposedly injured when the bomb went off just a few feet from her. Her shoe doesn't look like it has even been involved in the same crisis. This was on the video titled Boston Marathon bombing survivor killed. She was supposedly killed in a car accident overseas. Not sure if we will find out later she never died, but was doing a crisis over seas.

There is Bruce Mendelsohn who stated he was one or two blocks away from the bombing when it knocked him out of his seat. So did it physically blow him out of his seat or did he get startled and jump out voluntarily? Americans want to know the truth, just like when news commentators report the news and stage their backgrounds to appear somewhere else.

In this one video clip two reporters are talking back and forth as though they are both in completely different locations. However the vehicles in the background show a different scenario where at best they are a hundred feet from each other. True fakery at its worst. This was done and is on the link I have included in this book. All you need to do is check out these links and make your own educated decision.

There was Charles Jacobs, news reporter who too faked his location and reported on a story where he never was, this was posted on August 27, 2009 and was part of CNN. I had to laugh at the antics they used while reporting as one person puts on a helmet and the other one puts on a gas mask. It is obvious they never thought this through if there is a chemical attack the guy with the helmet is in trouble. They also point out the blue screen which is used like a green screen in editing, letting you be placed anywhere in the world while in one room.

In my Changing America books I had brought up Hillary Clinton being a survivor of sniper fire that never happened, that she said did, till she was caught in a lie and then wanted to blame it on sleep deprivation.

Maybe that is what the news media has when they report things that aren't real. The news media should be held accountable for all it reports, and to correct itself as soon as they catch their own mistakes or others bring it to their attention. This is where accountability becomes an important tool with policing our Truth Sayers, or those portraying the truth as respected news media, politicians and other officials that Americans look up to.

Remember at the beginning of the marathon FBI agents were spotted on top of buildings and had bomb sniffing dogs present as they were telling the people they had nothing to worry about that this was a training exercise.

There are a lot of red flags that are waving at us in this horrific event, but nothing points to just one person but a mass of different people at different levels throughout our country. We do need to be vigilant, when it comes to the next crisis. We need to look at each event as who has the motive, means, and opportunity to do these things. We need to look at those who will be the victims and those who will play the part of the predator and follow their history to see if anything stands out.

Since we have identified a few heroes for you, it seems only fair we go into the next story covering a hero we all know BATMAN, as we get ready to look at the Batman Shooting that happened in the theater in Aurora.

When only truth is spoken, lies cannot be heard.

Batman Theater Shooting

During the midnight hour on July 20,2012, at the Century 16 movie theater in Aurora, Colorado. The movie *The Dark Knight Rises,* is about to get real. A villain dressed in tactical gear tosses out tear gas and starts firing into the theater leaving seventy people injured and 12 dead.

It was noted as, one of the largest casualty shooting in the U.S. The villain was identified as James Eagan Holmes, who was arrested in his vehicle in the parking lot moments later. He also had rigged his home with explosives that were defused through the next few days after the shooting.

Holmes confessed to the shooting, but pled not guilty by reason of insanity. The prosecution sought the death penalty. On April 27, 2015. He was convicted of twenty four counts of first degree murder, along with 140 counts of attempted first degree murder, as well as possession of explosives, on July 16, 2015.

On August 7, 2015 he was sentenced to life in prison without the possibility of parole. On August 26,2015 he was given twelve life sentences, one for each person he killed and 3,318 years for the attempted murders of those he wounded, along with rigging the explosives in his home. News 9 reports that James Eagan Holmes, purchased 6,000 rounds of ammunition over the internet. They mentioned he had bought four guns in the last sixty days. The news announcer from News9 on CBS, Adele Arakawa, was the reporter covering this story.

Some of the victims were being treated for shrapnel and buck shot, while others had come into contact with the gas that was tossed in on them. They point out the weapons used were, AR15 assault rifle, 40 caliber Glock pistol, and a Remington shotgun. Looks like they have covered all the guns, along with the explosives.

They mention that James was wearing body armor from head to toe. He was wearing a ballistic helmet and vest, ballistic leggings, and throat protector, along with a gas mask. If we look at this alone, it would make you wonder why he had all that on if he is claiming insanity. Sounds like he thought it out and was well prepared.

Pierce O'Farrill was one of the victims of the shooting, he stated he saw him pull out the shotgun clear as day as he fired on the front rows he fired and lit up the theater. Pierce stated he appeared very methodical and never heard a single word out of him. He said James Eagan Holmes turned the gun on him and his friend and shot, hitting them both and then he was shot a second time. Pierce O'Farrill laid motionless hoping for dead. Pierce stated James was standing over him, he could feel his boot right next to his head.

Pierce stated he would be praying for James Eagan Holmes, this is less than twenty four hours after the shooting. This statement makes me think of Robbie Parker from the Sandy Hook school shooting, who stated pretty much the same thing.

A Connecticut man, Steven Bartman was a victim of the shooter and shared similar forgiveness to the shooter as well.

Rebecca Wingo and Marcus Weaver were there at the time of the shooting as well. They supposedly got separated in the chaos and Marcus went outside to get help and when he returned, stated he didn't know what happened to Rebecca.

The news caster reported that the pentagon reported four members of the armed forces were there as well. Alex Sullivan was one of the victims that died

The news reported that five nearby buildings have been evacuated, as they describe in their words bizarre items found in the home of James Eagan Holmes. Items that look like mortar shells, jars of ammo, jars of unidentified liquid with wires connected. All this making the insanity plea a little less convincing.

The families in the nearby buildings were forced to stay away till the band had been lifted. The Red Cross was on sight to assist , and stated they could help around 200 people.

Eric Kahnert, a news anchorman on News 9, reported law enforcement had said that James Eagan Holmes colored his hair red calling himself the joker. He is not cooperating with law enforcement other than saying his place is rigged with explosives.

The thought of a conspiracy arises in this case for a few reasons, as we go over these reasons keep an open mind. Look at all the evidence and remember the stories we have already covered. To me nothing is implausible.

James Eagan Holmes parked his vehicle outside the emergency exit. He then waited for the movie to start and went outside the emergency exit from inside the theater propping the door open. He then put on his gear then came back in tossing two gas canisters and shooting the first shot in the air. From here he started shooting randomly but methodically, as he was walking up the aisle. If we reenact this event according to the time, what will we see?

At 12:05 a man in the front row stood up pretending to take a phone call he went and opened the emergency exit stepping outside. Witnesses said he threw a green canister releasing smoke. At 12:30 am he returned wearing all his gear through the same exit he just went out. He then enters through the same door he left where he tosses in two canisters and shoots once in the air before unloading on the people.

If we look just at this time frame, we have to ask is it possible that people would stay inside the theater once the smoke was thrown for twenty five minutes? I have been around smoke and even smoke will affect you especially in a closed environment. Is it not interesting that when he went out the emergency exit an alarm never went off and no employee checked the door to see what is the problem?

The shooter had the ability to stage his vehicle gather his gear yet took him twenty five minutes? He pretended he was on a call as he was going out the emergency exit, but throws a canister of smoke taking away the purpose of pretending you are on a phone. What if the phone call was the trigger that made him follow through with this?

Who was on the other end of the phone call? Did they look in to this? Police Chief Dan Oates stated there was just one shooter, yet over the police scanners they mention a subject wearing a white and blue plaid shirt 3 minutes later. They also mention the canisters didn't come from the same directions, which could only mean another involved. There was a second gas mask found nearby as well, was it ever checked for DNA?

We also have to ask how twelve people were killed and fifty eight others approximately injured by a semi automatic weapon that jammed?

James's father worked for San Diego based HNC Software Incorporated. This company worked with DARPA to develop cortronic neural networks that enable machines to translate aural and visual stimuli and simulate humane thinking.

Does this not make you think of JADE II? His grandfather, Lt. Col. Robert Holmes was a graduate Turkish Language of the Army language school. He later was a graduate of the Defense Language Institute, in Monterey, California. The same military installation where Saeed Alghamdi trained, who was one of the alleged hijackers of 9/11.

They point out how the alleged gunman can't remember anything and how brain washing these subjects through drug induced states, using the example of Sirhan, Sirhan They once again focus on the guns and gun control rather than the shooter, or shooters. Almost every story we have covered so far has involved guns, or the temporary control of civilians.

FEMA EXPOSED

Talking about control of civilians, let's look at FEMA and what it has that might concern us. Let us start off with the conspiracy of the FEMA coffins. In the fall of 2000 a man had found in Madison, Georgia. An area that once was a soy bean field with a newly made road dividing the field, on the right side were these black containers. This man by the way drove trucks and had parked near these containers.

A vehicle pulled up next to his and it happened to be the property owner. The truck driver asked the owner what these boxes were, after realizing they were not port a potties. The owners statement was according to the trucker was, if he told him he would be one of few people in Madison that knew about them. He stated they're disposable coffins. He said there were 125,000 there at that time stacked fifteen high. He stated the CDC (Centers for Disease Control) owned them and that they were leasing his land for storage. He stated his brother worked for the CDC and was asked to do a three year extension to place temporary morgues all across the nation.

In January of 2005 the narrator doing this video decided to go and check out this area himself. He said it was on a Sunday and no one was around, with the exception of this one pickup truck that was coming out the one road they were going in on. They flagged down this truck, to find out he was the Son of the man who owned this field. The Son said there had been up to 500,000 here. He gave them permission to look around, so that is what they did.

On the video you see the man lying in the coffin, or what they call casket liners. The casket liners however are bigger than your average coffin, which tells me it is a basic cheap coffin used to stuff many bodies in rather than one body per container. The coffins lids were also flat so they could be easily stacked, keeping more containers in a tighter area, while saving space.

The man on the video, Dale Bohannon had mentioned that he went to a fund raiser. There were between 100 and 150 people, Congressmen's, Senators, Mayors, two and three star Generals, a couple one star Generals with their spouses.

The speaker was a congressman who was the Chairman of the Armed Services Committee, who spoke for or on behalf of Congressman Chambliss.

Dale Bohannon commented on them bringing up concerns of nuclear devices that were missing from the old Soviet Union that had gotten in to the hands of the terrorists. He stated that we could lose tens of millions of people in the next decade, due to a nuclear strike on the US soil. What would make them think we were in danger unless they knew something? Let's move on to another gentleman and hear what he has to say that will send chills down your back.

George Green, former investment banker mentions the manipulation of money to put people further in debt and the illusion in equity in real estate, which is coming apart. The players that are analyzing this are expecting massive foreclosures next year.

George Green said they had discussions stating there are just too many people on the planet referring to what Kissinger had stated. George mentioned two billion of us live on less than two dollars a day. George Green commented that these people are going to make God like decisions on who lives and who dies.

He had mentioned he sat in on these meetings and they had talked about using neutron bombs in major cities. He said he was making such a mess rather than kill him which they could have, they offered him the opportunity to join them instead. They asked him to be the Finance Chairman. He had mentioned he could have been Secretary of Treasure or whatever they wanted to do with him. He stated he volunteered to become president of a company and then he would liquidate it and get rid of the expendable containers, referring to people.

George Green said that they believed biological was much cheaper. He said, "They are still planning too, their plan is to get a war started in the middle East and they are still planning on using one of the bombs they still have on Israel, that's to begin World War III."

If we ask, who are these people that get to make these decisions as we sit idly by? I know we sit at home hearing these things and not wanting to believe our own country would kill, harm, or lie to us. Look at what is going on right now in our country with electing a new president. The people have spoken and it is not what the elite want so they are creating chaos to get the results they want. Manipulating, rules, stories, and people. The government is suppose to work for us not us for them.

George Green did mention Homeland Security, or FEMA if you want to call it that. He referred to them as one agency. George states they are going to shut everything down, his CIA friends, which he mentioned he wouldn't even call them his friends any more. He referred to the CIA as crooks in action. George mentioned even the CIA are concerned, and that they're leaving the country too, going to Latin America.

George Green stated they are working right now on prison of war camps, here in our country and mentioned a book he published, a book called *Chaos in America*. In the book he mentions he was asked to build a prisoner of war camp, right in downtown Las Vegas near the railroad tracks. He said enemy prison of war camp, putting emphasis on enemy, and they are building them all across the United States. He states Busch signed an executive order taking the old forts and Army places to get them organized to hold the so called dissidents.

The definition of dissident is, a person who opposes official policy, especially that of an authoritarian state.

He mentions that we are going to walk ourselves into these prisoner of war camps on our own and then they will go into the extermination process like in World War II.

There are underground FEMA bases that already exist George Green mentioned over a hundred of them. He stated in a question, "What you going to do with the rest of the people? Keep them above ground and they just get radiated." His son he mentioned is a Nuclear Physicist and spent the last three years in a secret city in Russia.

George mentioned that they, referring to Russia are about twelve years ahead of us. They have about 22,000 nuclear warheads, of course we're their target. The Soviets have three nuclear subs on the West coast and Three on the East coast. They are about two football fields in length and about five stories tall.

George Green mentioned they are not worried about him talking about this, after all they think there is nothing anyone can do. He mentioned China as well. With one billion three hundred million people, a little over four times our population. He stated he had played the game, and walked the talk. He stated, "I used to play around with the world leaders, so I know what they are planning on doing.

He was asked what happened to him to make him change his ways? He stated "It come back to a moral situation that happened to me I think. When I went to Aspen, I brought my two daughters up there so they could go skiing. When I went to this meeting, they asked me if I want to be the Finance Chairman for the President of the United States? I asked why me and they said we owe you a favor. Remember I told you I volunteered to be President of these companies, I didn't charge them anything for it, to me it was just a game."

George said during their meeting, he asked who was going to be president? He stated this was two years before the man did become president, Jimmy Carter, who was Democratic Governor of Georgia. George mentioned he was a Republican. They said don't worry about it we control both. This statement by itself makes you think about why everyone is against Donald Trump.

George asked what does a Finance Chairman do? He said he was told to sit down with Ted Kennedy, so he did. He stated, Ted Kennedy told him he was going to send him out to all these national Democratic functions to raise money for the Democratic party and you will meet some real foxy ladies. Just then his daughter walked in and Ted said "WOW" I want to go to bed with that. George said no you don't that's my daughter and she's fourteen. His response to George Green was I don't care. He said he was livid and that was part of the reason. He stated he then got up and walked across the room to talk with the Prime Minister of Canada at the time. He said he was sitting in front of them with a little cigar box full of white powder.

He said it just hit him all of a sudden, yet it didn't seem to bother him to look at people like a slaughter house he said you get to the point where people are just animals. What type of people have we created to lose sight of the humanistic values we were born with?

This next video clip starts off with this saying by John Hancock, "Resistance to Tyranny becomes the Christian and social duty of each individual. Continue steadfast and with a proper sense of your dependence on God, nobly defend those rights heaven gave, an no man ought to take from us."

We are here on this earth and alongside our friends as well as our enemies, because of God's generosity. He has given us everything we need to survive in peace and harmony, yet at times we must battle our enemies both foreign and domestic.

FEMA (Federal Emergency Management Agency) can be traced back to disaster legislation passed in 1803 to provide assistance to a New Hampshire town. Many, many years later, President Jimmy Carter signed Executive order 12127 during his term in office, emerging at least ten federal agencies into one, known now as FEMA.

In March 2003 FEMA joined twenty two other federal agencies to become part of Homeland Security. In 2005 when Hurricane Katrina hit New Orleans the people who couldn't get out of the area were directed, or encouraged to go to the superdome where there would be assistance to take care of them. As we look at the governments control through executive orders like the following.

Executive Order 10990, which allows the government to take over all modes of transportation and control of highways and seaports.

Executive Order 10995, allows the government to seize and control the communication media.

Executive Order 10997 allows the government to take over all electrical, power, gas, petroleum, fuels and minerals.

Executive Order 10998 allows the government to seize all means of transportation, including personal cars, trucks, or vehicles of any kind and total control over all highways, seaports, and waterways.

Executive Order 10999 allows the federal government to take over all food resources and farms.

Executive Order 11000 allows the government to mobilize civilians into work brigades under government supervision.

Executive Order 11001 allows the government to take over all health, education, and welfare functions.

Executive Order 11002 designates the Postmaster General to operate a national registration of all persons.

Executive Order 11003 allows the government to take over all airports and aircraft, including commercial aircraft.

Executive Order 11004 allows the Housing and Finance Authority to relocate communities, build new housing with public funding, designate areas to be abandoned, and establish new locations for populations.

Executive Order 11005 allows government to take over railroads, inland waterways, and public storage facilities.

Executive Order 11051 specifies the responsibility of the Office of Emergency Planning and gives authorization to put all executive orders into effect in times of increased international tensions and economic financial crisis.

If we look closer at these executive orders we will see we are the intended target.

Through these executive orders we lose control of our free movement from town to town, from State to State, or even from one country to the next. We lose our ability to communicate as well by letting the government dictate what they want you to think is happening and what they don't want you to know through the news media.

It appears this is already in effect. As we watch the news cover some of these stories, we have already discussed, and how the stories don't seem to add up. These executive orders cover our everyday life giving total control to the government. During 9/11 We saw that the airports were all shut down. We see that they are now looking to have all females register right alongside the males under the selective services. Whether it will get done is not yet known.

Some of this information came from the Alex Jones show. He has many more videos out there that you should watch as well. I think the internet is the one area they haven't yet mastered control of.

The next video talks about the homeless, but not helping the homeless, only controlling them by placing them in FEMA camps, or go to jail. Is there a difference between the two? Jail is for those that have been convicted of committing crimes. FEMA is supposedly taking the homeless placing them out of the way so they will not be a problem. Is this really going on? All we have to do is the math to see if two plus two equal four.

America has gone to war many times to protect its people, values, and land, but now for the first time we may have to battle from within our own borders.

In June of 2009 unemployment reported 467,000 jobs had been lost. Is this due to no work being available? Do the children of today think they are entitled to the same benefits without having to work?

When I grew up they had programs to help the unfortunate temporarily, like food stamps. Most were ashamed to be on them and got off them as quick as they could. While they appreciated them being there in a time of need, no one ever intended to live on those benefits. Today however many do think they are entitled.

We live in a society that makes our children believe no one loses. We hand out trophies to sympathize, rather than reward for the hard work one put in to come in first place. Is this all part of the plan to tear down those who strive for success by showing that all are equal at the end?

All we have to do is look at how people think to see things are different today than they were thirty years ago. Everyone is offended by something making us neutral to our own individuality, to fear expressing our own selves, in fear of hurting someone else.

RFID CHIP

Radio Frequency Identification Chip uses electromagnetic fields to automatically identify and track items that have been tagged. The tags contain electronically stored information Passive tags collect energy from a nearby RFID reader's interrogating radio waves. Active tags have a local power source and may operate at hundreds of meters from the RFID reader.

On Fox news they covered the RFID Chip and noted the inventor of the chip is from Saudi. It was designed to track terrorists and criminals. It not only has a GPS tracking system, but has a dose of cyanide that can be activated at any time, according to the news man on FOX news. The FOX spokesman reported that Germany is not allowing it. They mentioned it could be used to track illegal immigrants, political opponents, anyone that they deemed fit to monitor.

We need to remember just because you do not see it, doesn't mean it is not there. This goes with everything we have talked about, especially Jade II.

The Washington State legislator is right now considering registering 100 sex offenders with a GPS Chip that is implanted in their shoulder, because some have been wearing them on their wrists and have cut them off.

It is being presented as a good thing as they point out it can be used to track those with Alzheimer's, as well as track bad guys so they can't hide. The bad thing will be when everyone has to wear one and your right to plead the fifth will no longer matter because your chip would tell all. They point out that they will shut off your chip and when you go to run they will release the cyanide. This video was done back in 2010, six years earlier then this book was written.

In Reston, Virginia at South Lakes High School a town hall meeting was going on, and was being recorded on C-SPAN. A question that came up from a young lady, not really sure of her age, but am sure she would like to be seen as young. She asked the question, about some of their friends having a medical card and on the card it had a chip on it that held all their medical records from birth to whatever age they are. She was concerned with the government knowing all of their business from cradle to grave. She mentioned it was not about whether you were Republican or Democrat, but about your privacy between the patient and the doctor and shouldn't be shared with the government.

She had asked under what moral jurisdiction the constitution allows you to do that?.

The question was then directed to Dr. Howard Dean.

Dr. Howard Dean was the former governor of Vermont and the Democratic National Committee Chairman. He admitted this was a huge issue and that it is more than just health care. He pointed out that he understood why people are not so sure about the government, insurance, and banks knowing all of their information, and then it being sent to all these credit card companies and you then get all their junk mail.

Dr. Howard Dean then states we all want to see patients get quality care and the complete medical attention possible. This allows a person hundred miles away who needs medical attention the ability to have his medical records right there with him, all they have to do is plug in the card into the computer.

He points out the guards are, a bill that was passed called, HIPAA (Health Insurance Portability and Accountability Act). Dr. Howard Dean stated the problem is this was not enough, referring not just to the government, but the private sector as well. He pointed out just the other day from when this meeting was taking place a hacker had gotten in and stole 130 million credit card numbers. These are the things Americans are concerned with, plus finding the right balance between government and the private sector. Unfortunately there is no perfect answer according to Dr. Howard Dean.

The other Representative that was there was Jim Moran, D.- Virginia 8th District.

NBC news reported that in the year 2017 our world would be different as what was once seen as science fiction, would become biometric reality of today. It is currently 2016 and we seem to already be there with the RFID chip.

We have finger prints and Iris scans that are in use at some airports. We have cameras and software that are capable of doing facial recognition scanning millions of faces in a data base.

According to **Revelation 13:16 -18** "And he causeth all, both small and great, rich and poor, free and bond to receive a mark in their right hand, or their foreheads and that no man might buy or sell, save he that had the mark, or the name of the beast, or the number of his name."

If this catches your attention, great as we look at what the purpose of this chip is, we have to wonder if this is what the bible warned us of. We see that these chips are being used for tracking purposes, along with gaining entrance through certain doors as you can see on the video. They show people that have already been chipped using their hand to access merchandise. This could be seen as the sign of the beast, what you do with this knowledge will, or could decide your fate.

There are already doors that will unlock deadbolts by the use of finger prints, the same with purchasing items at certain stores, merely by using your finger print over a scanner. They bring up the movie Minority Report as a prime example of the future that's becoming reality. It appears we are slowly being programmed through movies and every day conveniences that we take for granted. Let's move on and see what else we have in store for you.

In 2005 an agreement between Canada, TheUnited States, and Mexico was made. This arrangement merged the three countries into one entity. It is called the North American Union. President Busch signed a formal agreement that will end the United States as we know it. The decision to ignore the open border policy and enforcement there along with illegal immigration laws.

This was done without the approval of congress, or the people of the United States. This was reported on CNN, as they stated it was a total removal of sovereignty from these three countries. This also brought up the unification of our three countries currency, calling it the amero. It focuses on these three countries having no borders between them much like what they have in Europe.

They mention on CNN that this treaty will end our constitution as we know it. They point out that the North American Union is the same as the European Union, African Union, and the soon to be Asian Union. They state they are all part of the same group of people that are behind each of these unions, and when it is all said and done they will once again merge into one, making a one world government.

Paul Warburg, Council on Foreign Relations and architect of the Federal reserve system stated. "We shall have World Government whether or not we like it. The only question is whether World Government will be achieved by conquest or consent."

Let us continue as we listen to what Aaron Russo had to say. Aaron Russo, a film maker and former politician who had met with Nicholas Rockefeller of the infamous banking and business dynasty. They became friends until Aaron ended their close friendship, after learning about what the Rockefeller's ambitions were.

Aaron stated that Nicholas had mentioned there was going to be an event, eleven months before 9/11 attack. He said out of this event, you are going to see that we're going to go in to Afghanistan, so we can run pipe lines into the Caspian Sea. We are going to go into Iraq to take the oil and establish a base in the Middle East. We are going to go into Venezuela and try and get rid of Hugo Chavez, who happened to be the 64th President of Venezuela. He mentioned they were going to go in to caves looking for people they were never going to find.

He stated Rockefeller said, "By having this war on terror you can never win it. You can continue to take peoples liberties away." Aaron stated he asked how will you convince people it's real? He stated, "The media can convince everybody that it's real."

Aaron asked him why he was doing all this for, he had all the money you could want? Why are you hurting people? Supposedly Rockefeller's response was, "Worry about yourself and your family." His ultimate goal is to get everybody chipped with the RFID chip. "If they don't do what we want we just turn off their chip." It is interesting how everything comes back to being controlled. Americans need to cut the strings, we don't have to be their puppets.

In 2005, Congress under the pretense of immigration control, and the so called war on terrorism, passed the REAL ID, which was projected by May of 2008 you would be required to carry around a Federal Identification card, which includes a scanned bar code with your personal information. This is the first step however towards getting us closer to their ultimate goal of the RFID chip.

Yes it is currently 2016 and I am still not aware of the REAL ID card. This doesn't mean it is not out there in our Illinois FOID (Firearms Owner Identification) cards. It could be in all our State drivers licenses. Maybe they are implementing it in our vehicles using the well known ON STAR. It can locate your vehicle, unlock your vehicle, and shut off your vehicle from anywhere.

We have cell phones with GPS, again you can be tracked along with being recorded where you have been by mapping backwards your GPS locations. They now have the attractive FITBIT watches. These watches monitor your sleep, how often you wake, when you wake, heartbeat, steps, how many calories you burned. These watches let you know when someone is calling you and have caller ID on them. The FITBIT watches are being implemented like our phones through attractiveness and conveniences. Why try and jeopardize that by forcing you to carry a REAL ID card when you can be subtle and accomplish it by having the people come to you for these items?

A coyote doesn't always attack directly, but through deception as they lure their prey in to its final killing field.

They report the RFID chip is already in all new passports that are being issued. The chip itself is no bigger than a grain of rice. If they can get you to just think it as the norm you will then just fall in with all the other sheep that are on their way to being slaughtered. I don't see any other way of explaining it. Many including myself see this as more than a chip. It is giving up not just your human freedom but your spiritual freedom pulling you away from God.

I am not the smartest person in the world, but if I can see deception as the tool of their choice verse force and defiance, don't you think they would be able to see this as well? If you were to sell a glass bowl or plate and it was chipped it wouldn't be worth as much, maybe that is the lesson once we are chipped we become worthless for we have turned away from God. As we continue on let us look at those that are associated with the Illuminati.

ILLUMINATI

Illuminati refers to various organizations which claim to have connections to the original Bavarian Illuminati, which was founded on May 1st 1776 or similar secret societies. Their purpose was to oppose superstition, obscurantism, religious influence over public life, and abuses of State power.

The Illuminati, along with Free Masonry and other secret societies were outlawed through edict by the Bavarian ruler, Charles Theodore with the encouragement of the Roman Catholic church in 1784, 1785, 1787, and 1790.

Conservative and religious critiques claimed they continued underground, and were responsible for the French Revolution.

The Illuminati through various secret societies teach intellect, technology, and science, giving man the belief he will achieve immortality. Satan was implying that secret wisdom and information would be available to those that would submit to the ones who hold the knowledge. They believe that man is spiritually evolving into a spiritual higher consciousness. They see themselves as Gods, as they will acquire power, authority, and dominion over the masses while conquering death and nature. This is the core to the Luciferian doctrine.

There is also Alice Bailey who wrote in the book, *The Externalization of the Hierarchy*. She stated "Christianity must also be overthrown because it is based on Jewish sources; the rule of Christ must come to an end, because only the rule of force is right. In the world order of axis powers, the individual has no rights; he has no freedom except in so far as he serves the state." This is on page 101 of the above titled book.

There is Albert Pike the Author of *Morals and Dogma*. Who stated, "The Teachers of even Christianity, are, in general the most ignorant of the true meaning of that which they teach. There is no book of which so little is known as the Bible. To most who read it, it is as incomprehensible as the Sohar." This was on page 109 of *Morals and Dogma*.

Many think the Illuminati is just a figment of imagination. Seek out that which is fact or fiction.

Greg Szymanski, is one who has investigated conspiracies. He interviewed a woman called Svalli, who is an ex-Illuminati and now Christian. He interviewed her on a radio talk show. Some of what she said will send chills down your spine. She talked about the Vatican and going down underneath the Vatican in the depths of darkness.

She was young at the time and was born into the Illuminati through wealthy parents. She was born in Germany. By the time she was a teenager she was a youth leader. All members go through training under different degrees, depending on their role. When she was twenty two years old she became the youngest member of leadership council in San Diego County. She states she was the head trainer. She stated, "When I was twelve I went through the ceremony at the Vatican, which they make all leadership in the group under go at some point."

Svalli mentioned she was briefed on what she was expected to do while she was in Germany, as they prepared her for a couple days beforehand. She stated, "We went to the Vatican. Underneath the Vatican there is a large room I described to you, that we talked on before. It had thirteen catacomb chambers leading into it. What they do is as you go down the steps into the room, you can see they're all circular, they are all rounded. They bring out the mummies from the catacombs and set them by each one. They say that is the spirits from the fathers watching over the ceremony and there was a large table in the center of the room it was on top of this huge pentagram. They had a ceremony there."

She was asked how many other kids were there being inducted into the group?

She states there were two other children at that time, and several adults too. Svalli stated they bring in adults, to swear allegiance as well. She stated what she had witnessed was the following, " There was a table in the middle looked like glass, it was very shiny and looked black and looked like onyx, I'm not sure, it was the only type of stone like that. Around the corners they had these like gold channels that collect fluids. There was a little boy sitting on the table on drugs. I think he was on drugs because he was very quiet, he didn't move or say anything."

She stated he was a little three or four year old boy. She stated they continued to do a human, or child sacrifice. Svalli stated she was absolutely horrified, and was just hoping it would all get over quickly. She had mentioned the one who did the sacrifice was in scarlet color and spoke in Latin saying please accept this sacrifice. Svalli stated "I had to go before this man who wore this big gold ring and kneel and kiss his ring. I had to swear my allegiance to him and the New World Order, until my death. They also said may the same occur, or worse occur to you should you ever break this oath."

The Free Masons say the same thing in their ceremony as well. Let's get back to Svalli who did mention this was all being performed under the Vatican. The Vatican is one of the most sacred and powerful places in the world. Let's look at the Vatican closer.

The Vatican is a city with in a city, it is inside Rome, Italy. It is approximately 110 acres, with a population of 842. It has a wall that goes around its own city, with its own police. This is the city of the Pope. It is said to be one of the wealthiest places in the world. Vatican City is currently the only widely recognized independent state that has not become a member of the United Nations.

I was privileged to visit the Vatican during my Marine Corp tour, while assigned to the USS. Puget Sound. We were given a special tour of the facility by the Pope's own guards, the Swiss Guards. We toured the Sixteenth Chapel. I remember being told of old books connected to the Bible that were being stored and guarded. To hear of such evil, the sacrificing of a young child's life right under such a Holy city, makes me cringe.

What is really weird is while I am writing on this subject, I am contacted by one of my fellow Marines from the very same detachment I was in at the time I was discussing. I think God is telling me he has my back. This was over thirty years ago when I was stationed on the USS Puget Sound.

As we move on to our next area of deception, know God is with you, and that everything happens for a reason. I am not trying to change the theme of this book, but is it possible that all these events could be connected in a manner that will make us cry out to God?

JOHN F. KENNEDY

The story of John F. Kennedy's assassination is probably one of the most famous conspiracy stories ever. On a Friday afternoon in Dallas, Texas November 22, 1963, President John F. Kennedy was assassinated by gunfire as his motorcade drove slowly down the street in Dallas as he sat in an open unprotected limousine.

Two hours after the assassination Lee Harvey Oswald was arrested for the murder of Dallas police officer, J.D. Tippit and arraigned that evening. Sometime after 1:30 am on Saturday morning he was arraigned for the murder of President Kennedy as well.

Texas Governor John Connally was wounded during the assault on Kennedy, as he rode along as a passenger in the car. In 1973 Connally switched parties going from Democrat to Republican and in 1980 tried running unsuccessfully as the Republican nominee. There were five government investigations that were done and they all pointed at Lee Harvey Oswald as the shooter who killed Kennedy.

Lee Harvey Oswald was an American Sniper, that was identified as killing President Kennedy. He was a former U.S. Marine who they state defected to the Soviet Union in October of 1959. He lived in the Belarusian city of Minsk until June of 1962, at which time he returned to the U.S. with his Russian wife and settled in Dallas, Texas.

Lee Harvey Oswald denied shooting anybody and stated he was their patsy. Two days later while Oswald was being transferred from the police headquarters to the county jail, he himself became the victim as he was shot and mortally wounded by Dallas night club owner, Jack Ruby in full view of the media, during a live broadcast.

In 1964 the Warren Commission concluded that Oswald acted alone, firing three shots at the President. The Federal Bureau of Investigation, Secret Service, and the Dallas Police Department all substantiated the Warren Commission's findings.

Despite forensic, ballistic, and eye witnesses supporting the one shooter theory, many people believe that Oswald didn't act alone. They believe a conspiracy involving multiple people took place. Americans would love to trust our government, but as you can see in these more recent events that our government seems to be the chef that's stirring the pot. I know there has been hundreds of stories done on the JFK assassination, I am just pointing out some of the basic discrepancies that I have found through others findings. Things that make you think and ponder why, or what if. Let us look at some of these and see where they may go.

Dr. Malcolm Perry was an American physician and surgeon, who happened to attend to the President of the United States, John F. Kennedy at Parkland Memorial hospital in Dallas, Texas. The Doctor had reportedly stated the bullet came from the front. He was trained in treating trauma patients and bullet wounds.

Lee Harvey Oswald gun, was a 6.5mm. Mannlicher-Carcano, which was not a high powered rifle and was identified as extremely inaccurate. With the telescopic scope on the rifle the shooter would have had to reposition the rifle after each shot due to the massive recoil.

During Oswald's time as a Marine, he only qualified as a marksman. This is the lowest level award given to a Marine who qualifies. Starting with Marksman, then Sharpshooter, then Expert. He was a radar technician learning Russian, which operate, install, calibrate, and maintain integrated computer/ communications systems, consoles, simulators, and other data acquisition, test, and measurement instruments and equipment. They state with his knowledge it would have been virtually impossible for him to fire those three shots in 6.3 seconds.

The experts that the Warren Commission hired were unable to complete the task as well. The key word was experts.

Ten squad cars along with the Media, showed up at the local movie theater to arrest Oswald, they didn't know if he would be there or not. A worker supposedly informed the law enforcement agency that a man had entered without purchasing a ticket.

Everette Howard Hunt, an intelligence officer with the CIA, along with other government officials supposedly came clean stating the operation to kill Kennedy was code named **The Big Event**.

Lee Harvey Oswald was interrogated approximately twelve hours. During the interrogation no video was recorded, making what could appear as hard evidence, only then becomes speculation, and trusting the very people everybody was suspicious of from the start. The notes that were taken were later destroyed, why? They state he was denied legal representation, even though he asked to see a lawyer.

The Lincoln Limousine, which John F. Kennedy was shot in was in Detroit being refurbished the Monday after the assassination, on November 25, 1963. Forensics were not even done on the limousine, before it was being cleaned, or evidenced manipulated.

Lee Harvey Oswald's alleged gun was found hidden on the sixth floor of the Texas school book suppository by investigators. The rifle was swept for prints, with several prints being found. The investigation concluded under six grooves resembled Oswald's. According to the Federal law at that time, six to twelve need to be in relations to the defendants for it to be used in court.

Oswald never made it to court as he was assassinated himself by Jack Ruby. If you remember I had mentioned what doesn't make sense today may make sense tomorrow. If we look at the media as the tool of choice, we can see who the killer is, while we stop asking who could have done it. The problem then becomes why?

President Kennedy's body was illegally moved from Parkland memorial hospital in Dallas, to the Bethesda naval hospital by secret service agents before an autopsy was performed.

Elm street was the street Kennedy was killed on is a 120 degree turn. The standard secret service motorcade protocol was a maximum 90 degree turn.

The majority of people said that they heard the shot come from the front and right of the vehicle. They state this explains why his head goes back and to the left in the video, along with why agents headed in that direction looking for the shooter, or shooters. The video is clear the shot came from the right.

They mention the formation of the motorcade as they point out the President doesn't decide on the position of the security details, this is done by the secret service. The standard grouping used by the secret service is called the wedge position, which protects the President from all directions. The position they used was called the sitting duck formation. I think the definition speaks for itself, as we all bear witness to the end result.

Was this formation there to protect the President or ensure his death? Were the secret service all part of this, or was there a mixture of both those that knew and those that didn't? From that question you could then ask of how much loyalty would be needed if they did know of the conspiracy? They mention that test showed Oswald was telling the truth when he told the press he was just a patsy.

Paper trails along with family members confirm that Lee Harvey Oswald was in two different places at the same time. Many were aware that another person was using the same identity.

Lee Harvey Oswald had his tonsils removed as a child. When his body was later dug up it was found to still have tonsils remaining. This by itself ought to show something suspicious. As we move into new technology, we the public become just as smart and capable of using sophisticated tools that help us see things that once were hidden or for only the select few.

His wife said some of his scars that he once had were suddenly gone as she viewed his body during postmortem, again only adding more doubt to what others had claimed.

They mentioned the bullet fragments being inspected, those in or near Kennedy's body after being inspected they were astonished that no blood or flesh was found on any part of the ammunition. They pointed out the Blood and brain matter ejected from Kennedy's skull sprayed backwards, even ending up on the two police motorcycles.

They also confirmed that Jack Ruby and Lee Harvey Oswald knew each other. The Warren Commission either ignored this or lied about it stating there was no connection between the two.

Check out the Zapruder film. See what your eyes tell you. Everything means something, which is what this book is all about.

To expose the truth by questioning that which does not make sense, parents do this all the time with their children. It's funny that when we do the same in regards to our government we are looked upon as conspiracy theorists.

The Chief Counsel for the House of Assassinations Committee, Robert Blakey stated, that they made sure no secret service members were in that area, however others say there were people there with credentials, but they were not really who they said they were. This statement if nothing else should at least be looked at, even if it is unfounded.

They state the President would normally have his physician, along with his military aide who would carry the portable phone, so the President could stay in constant contact with the National Security Agency. On the day of the assassination these two men were excluded from the limousine.

In one of the video links I have provided here, they bring up the driver of the limousine, saying he was actually breaking as the shots were fired until he looked back and seen the target was eliminated. On the drivers defense, this was a one man parade. I have never seen anyone drive fast through a parade area. In the frame they show the driver clearly looking back as the narrator states twelve shots have already been fired. The President and Governor Connally have five wounds between them at this point. There is a hole in the windshield and he is still looking back. This is the reason that the behavior seems suspicious, it is as though he is waiting to make sure every attempt is given to eliminate the target.

They mention the word slump, as though it were a code word by the killers, used to take out the President. Governor Connally stated the following, while he was in the hospital.

"We had just turned the corner, we heard a shot, I turned and looked in the back seat and seen the President slumped, and he didn't say nothing. All of a sudden I turned and I was hit, I was hit bad."

Later while in Austin Texas he states the following. "When the first shot was fired I recognized it as a shot, I thought of nothing else but that of a rifle shot. I turned to my right, I had time to think I had time to react. I turned to my right and I looked over my right shoulder to see if I could see anything unusual, and particularly if I could protect the President, because I immediately thought it was an assassination attempt. I didn't see anything but a blur of people moving. I did not see anything unusual, I did not see the President out the corner of my eye. I was in the process of looking over my other shoulder."

It is interesting that his story changed from seeing the President to not seeing him. His second story too he tells in a commanding way as though he were aware of everything from the type of gun, that being a rifle. We must not forget Governor Connally is a politician, who is skilled with dancing with words.

I am sure even in the old days politicians were the same. I know in today's world we can challenge them better as we have the internet and video cameras out there collecting everything they say and do.

President Kennedy was murdered in Dallas, Texas, his body was taken by the secret service and loaded on Air Force One and flown back to Washington. David Lifton stated the President did not make an uninterrupted flight from Dallas to Bethesda.

Jessie Ventura wrote a book called, *They Killed Our President* It is a book with new information, along with being endorsed and talked about on INFO WARS. You can't look into conspiracies without at least listening to some of the topics discussed on that show.

While I know there is a lot of information out there on the Kennedy assassination, I am going to turn to some other conspiracies, as we leave this one with hundreds of books already done on this topic.

Heart Attack Gun

The Church committee hearings were begun due to the press bringing out concerns on legality with intelligence gathering of the CIA, NSA, and FBI. Senator Frank Church was the Chairman of the committee. This was in the early 1970's.

During the hearings they bring out a gun that was designed to shoot a dart like round, it was frozen and small, leaving just a small speck it would kill a person leaving them as though they died from a heart attack. It was designed to be shot into the person without their knowledge of being hit. The speed of the round would actually melt the round as it entered the body. The poison would be undetectable during an autopsy.

This gun did exist in the early 1970's over forty years ago. In their own words during the Church Committee Hearings they state this gun could shoot someone without their perception of being shot. I know you are wondering why would I bring this up now. As I have said throughout this book what doesn't make sense today may make sense tomorrow.

As we move forward, Supreme Court Justice Scalia, on February 13,2016 passed away. He was found dead at West Texas Ranch. He was on a getaway with high ranking members of an elite hunting and fraternity whose origins date back to 1695. Some of the thirty five members that were in attendance at the Cibolo Creek Ranch, were confirmed members of a secretive Austrian society, called the International Order of St. Hubertus.

While it is unclear Scalia's connection with the group, the owner of Cibolo Creek Ranch, John Poindexter and C Allen Foster a prominent lawyer were both leaders in the society.

It took hours after noticing the body to find a Justice of the Peace, and when they did, they reached them by phone. Presidio County Judge Cinderela Guevara, was the one who pronounced Scalia's death to be of natural cause without even seeing the body. This was done over the phone, which in Texas is legal, but to me not ethical, or professional. She did say her decision was based on the talking of law enforcement officers, who stated they seen nothing that warranted foul play. Justice Scalia's physician also mentioned he had numerous chronic conditions. I would want one done just to show he did die of natural causes, so later people like me don't make others wonder.

Judge Scalia was supposedly found dead by the owner John Poindexter, who became worried when Scalia didn't appear for breakfast that morning. The manager at an El Paso funeral home stated the family made it clear they did not want an autopsy done. Would we listen to a husband who says I don't want an autopsy done on my wife, we surely would not.

This event too, can go back to motive, means, and opportunity. He is a prominent Judge with lots of power and influence. The means as I brought up earlier is the heart attack gun that they had from forty years ago. I am sure it is more advanced now. Our forensics are more advanced now as well, which could have been our opportunity to find, or not find something.

We know he was a very important person, after all the President of the United States wanted to replace him as fast as possible, after the Judge's death and before the end of his term in office. Everyone knew he sat in a very vital spot, one that could dictate our constitutional rights and freedoms.

Supreme Court Justice Scalia was the key judge that defended our 2nd amendment, along with important issues like abortion, and Obama Care. He was the judge that tipped the scales for or against these important issues. He ends up dead and President Obama was quick to try and replace him. He didn't have the time to pay his respect to the judge, only time to select another that would fit his political agenda. Is it not plausible for us Americans to question this very president who drags his feet on everything that benefits America, and hurries to give our enemy everything they need to destroy us?

The famous news media, The National Enquirer,
exposes more information saying this was no accident,
but a political murder assassination, orchestrated by the
CIA and carried out by a $2000.00 hooker

A top Washington D.C. source, said the February
13,2016 death of seventy nine year old Justice Scalia was
part of a conspiracy that tracks back to the CIA and the
White House.

The insider reported a CIA operative hired a hooker
who apparently injected a poison into Scalia's buttocks.
Former Secret Service agent John A. Carman, supposedly
told the National Enquirer "This death has all the
markings of a political assassination."

Stating a needle was used and that she injected a
poison into him that would make it appear he died from a
heart attack, Wow interesting this was talked about clear
back in the Church Committee hearings. They also
mentioned a pillow was found over his head as he were
lying on his back. To me that screams foul play.

Former Criminal Investigator for Washington D.C's
Metropolitan Police Department, William O Ritchie,
commented according to the Washington Post, saying he
was stunned there was no autopsy done. Once again, a
top D.C. source stated to the National Enquirer, that they
feared a Republican would be elected to office in
November and that Antonin Scalia was killed because
they knew he would tip the scales towards the
conservatives. They also mentioned that he knew some of
the deepest darkest secrets of the Obama administration.

They state the body could have been flown back and properly investigated with a thorough autopsy, but instead was secretly transported to a funeral home off the beaten trail. The corpse was embalmed and fluids were disposed of, cleansing the body of other possible evidence that could have been examined for foul play.

Scalia had also decided to not have present his U.S. Marshall detail. The National Enquirer also stated a CIA spy was seen visiting a nearby whorehouse just across the Mexican border and that a mystery woman was caught on camera before his body was discovered. They mention the name of the drug that could have been used, calling it Succinylcholine.

If we look at the organization that was mentioned, the International Order of St. Hubertus. It is a worldwide organization and knightly order of hunters and wildlife conservationists that was founded in 1695. They promote hunting ethics, and practices. Franz Anton von Sporck was the founder he brought together noble hunters from other countries, such as Austria, and Bohemia. The Order was named in honor of Saint Hubertus, the patron saint of hunters and fishermen.

The Order's motto is *Deum Diligite Animalia Diligentes*, "Honoring God by Honoring His Creatures. As of 2011 the male only order, has 250 members from the United States and 600 members worldwide. It is a small group when we look at the vast amount of people in the world. On the other hand you have to look at quality over quantity, or the rich and famous over the not so rich and famous. I added these link pages just to make sure I did not miss anything important.

These links cover all the topics we have so far covered in this book. As we continue on we need to remember these events each represent a piece of the puzzle, or a part of the larger picture.

https://www.youtube.com/watch?v=X3aYQEJXJfo

https://www.youtube.com/watch?v=aQz1BIM9mLw

https://www.youtube.com/watch?v=oD0z275nQnM

https://www.youtube.com/watch?v=IV20DtXBuQs

https://www.youtube.com/watch?v=Hvhs5PWQW-o

https://www.youtube.com/watch?v=iCGDFUWVyG8

https://www.youtube.com/watch?v=3uZqtWWqD0E

https://www.youtube.com/watch?v=eYwPN5-FDoc

https://www.youtube.com/watch?v=ivt1KzZ9Bs8

https://www.youtube.com/watch?v=WmJO3ljBy7Y

https://www.youtube.com/watch?v=AUSJ6rqEWUY

https://www.youtube.com/watch?v=Q3tc4-qKvzw

https://www.youtube.com/watch?v=wGOuzeeSzUg

https://www.youtube.com/watch?v=K4310XOz4tc

https://en.wikipedia.org/wiki/Jade_Helm_15_conspiracy_th eories

https://www.youtube.com/watch?v=l3IhN7itG6Y

https://www.youtube.com/watch?v=Dhgrgf9sYK8

https://www.youtube.com/watch?v=7i1F8rL7rSk

https://www.youtube.com/watch?v=4L1IFoL08f0

https://www.youtube.com/watch?v=UusMk7JNmQs

https://www.youtube.com/watch?v=1zJ4DJOt5T0

https://www.youtube.com/watch?v=4Nmj6t51Wz8

https://www.youtube.com/watch?v=IL8cJWyOxWQ

https://www.youtube.com/watch?v=cHHghW4Pg5k

https://www.youtube.com/watch?v=YVDdjLQkUV8

https://www.youtube.com/watch?v=-Laaq44SDgg

https://www.youtube.com/watch?v=75Ja-W5LWVk

https://www.youtube.com/watch?v=YQBlv7sZGVE

https://www.youtube.com/watch?v=xsDBAixXJdM

https://www.youtube.com/watch?v=8xRaJ5QA1kk

https://www.youtube.com/watch?v=s3CGyH5ftdE

https://en.wikipedia.org/wiki/Waco_siege

https://www.youtube.com/watch?v=XreYBolUn7s

https://www.youtube.com/watch?v=zpeF2VXWVlk

https://www.youtube.com/watch?v=RrJewJPyptk

https://www.youtube.com/watch?v=l08zD9Pn1jk

https://www.youtube.com/watch?v=tT5PS_cljgo

https://www.youtube.com/watch?v=UpNIMSDwvOw

https://www.youtube.com/watch?v=_boRHcIKH6I

https://en.wikipedia.org/wiki/Boston_Marathon_bombing

https://www.youtube.com/watch?v=HS-1h9DDBrY

https://www.youtube.com/watch?v=2ACbRMMC-vI

https://www.youtube.com/watch?v=BLwRR5Z3CO8

https://www.youtube.com/watch?v=m88DgjsfgpE

https://www.youtube.com/watch?v=MiNOrkAyFBU

https://www.youtube.com/watch?v=c7XhubLFR6o

https://www.youtube.com/watch?v=8Pg62xyv1jE

https://www.youtube.com/watch?v=2hGZM7heYKw

https://www.youtube.com/watch?v=xs9rHYtAVN0

https://www.youtube.com/watch?v=PLlWV6UFF1U

https://en.wikipedia.org/wiki/2012_Aurora_shooting

https://www.youtube.com/watch?v=AIA5LsadeOo

https://www.youtube.com/watch?v=Ngha-LZRdvQ

https://www.youtube.com/watch?v=ZtjxEQNhsaw&ebc=AN
yPxKphlfNDIJMfXek3j1ZjQR5rHFSfsAhAUo1G0FneoCL4KLRV
OvqnUAixYR_m0uVm-1-Dp0mleSla2aUQ1vzUzetU1warnA

https://www.youtube.com/watch?v=AaZDc1RNmc4

https://www.youtube.com/watch?v=Tw6DiqpC4rl

https://www.youtube.com/watch?v=8TcMC7ZQ_6w

https://www.youtube.com/watch?v=hMui2n2KEus

https://www.youtube.com/watch?v=vn60K0CM_5w

https://www.bing.com/videos/search?q=rfid+chips+in+hum
ans&&view=detail&mid=A6C6022A42A6F5BA9B10A6C6022
A42A6F5BA9B10&FORM=VRDGAR

https://www.youtube.com/watch?v=vuBo4E77ZXo

https://www.youtube.com/watch?v=TCkmdUtZmdg

https://www.youtube.com/watch?v=TCkmdUtZmdg

https://www.youtube.com/watch?v=Sy_pvffqchk

https://en.wikipedia.org/wiki/Vatican_City

https://en.wikipedia.org/wiki/Lee_Harvey_Oswald

https://www.youtube.com/watch?v=qRnmoiXO7WE

This last chapter started off with The former President John F. Kennedy and we ended it with Supreme Court Justices Antonin Scalia. Both these gentlemen were well known, well liked, and both had adversaries, however the more powerful you are the higher the stakes become. Is it possible that they became obstacles to a greater cause, or is it just that we as humans seam skeptical of events that involve those of wealth and power?

Did these two hold secrets to die for?

America is a great country, though it is our leaders both those we see and those we don't that can make this country even greater. They need to remember this is not just their country but all of ours, and we are here to claim it.

THE NEW WORLD ORDER

This is where the elite families use their wealth and power to control events from behind the scenes. While many are unaware of a hidden agenda that is continuously growing right before our eyes.

In 1775 the American Revolution starts, the colonist fight for their beliefs and freedom. Now over 200 and some years later, we again are in a battle. Here every American will be fighting for their independence for their freedom. Is this just a rumor or story made to scare people? Are their people rich enough to sway others and control the world from behind the scenes?

Numerous Presidents have said the words **New World Order** in various speeches. A one ruled government where everyone unites as one and we all get along. The definition of getting a long may vary as some see the masses as slaves to the rich, where we become prisoners of our own making.

Who are these rich people that pull the strings from above? Many think they are part of a group, known as the Bilderberg group.

The **Bilderberg Group**, **Bilderberg conference**, **Bilderberg meetings**, or **Bilderberg Club** is an annual private conference of 120 to 150 people of the European and North American <u>political elite</u>, experts from industry, finance, academia, and the media, established in 1954. The following is a list of those that have attended from wikipedia.org.

- <u>Thomas E. Donilon</u> (2012),[3] Executive Vice President for Law and Policy at Fannie Mae (1999–2005), National Security Advisor (2010 – 2013)
- <u>Roger Altman</u> (2008, 2009, 2013),[2][12][103] Deputy Treasury Secretary from 1993–1994, Founder and Chairman of <u>Evercore Partners</u>
- <u>George W. Ball</u> (1954, 1993),[104] Under Secretary of State 1961–1968, Ambassador to U.N. 1968 (deceased)
- <u>Sandy Berger</u> (1999),[105] <u>National Security Advisor</u>, 1997–2001
- **<u>Hillary Rodham Clinton</u>** (1997),;[106] First Lady of the USA when attending, later 67th United States Secretary of State
- <u>Timothy Geithner</u> (2008, 2009),[2][103] <u>Treasury Secretary</u>
- **<u>Dick Gephardt</u>** (2012),[3] former <u>Congressman</u> and House Majority Leader
- <u>Lee H. Hamilton</u> (1997),[8][*better source needed*] former <u>Congressman</u>
- <u>Christian Herter</u>,[107] (1961, 1963, 1964, 1966), 53rd United States Secretary of State (deceased)

- Charles Douglas Jackson (1957, 1958, 1960),[108] Special Assistant to the President (deceased)
- Joseph E. Johnson[109] (1954), President Carnegie Endowment for International Peace (deceased)
- **Henry Kissinger** (1957, 1964, 1966, 1971, 1973, 1974, 1977, 2008, 2009, 2010,[23] 2011, 2012,[3] 2013,[12] 2015[14]),[72][110] 56th United States Secretary of State
- Mark G. Mazzie (1986, 1987),[3] Chief of Staff, The Honorable George C. Wortley, U.S. House of Representatives.
- Richard Perle (2011), Chairman of the Defense Policy Board Advisory Committee 2001–2003, United States Assistant Secretary of Defense 1981–1987[73]
- **Colin Powell** (1997),[8][better source needed] 65th United States Secretary of State
- **Condoleezza Rice** (2008),[2] 66th United States Secretary of State
- **George P. Shultz** (2008),[2] 60th United States Secretary of State
- Lawrence Summers,[103] Director of the National Economic Council
- Paul Volcker (2010),[103] Chair of the President's Economic Recovery Advisory Board and Chairman of the Federal Reserve from 1979–1987
- Terry Wolfe (2010),[23] author and former Assistant Secretary of Defense for International Security Affairs
- Robert Zoellick (2008–2015),[2][3][11][12][13][14][23][45] former Trade Representative, former Deputy Secretary of State and former President of the World Bank Group

Presidents

- George H.W Bush (1989,1992)[citation needed]
- Bill Clinton (1991),[97][98] President 1993–2001
- Gerald Ford (1964, 1966),[15][111] President 1974–1977 (deceased)

Senators

- Tom Daschle (2008),[2] Senator from South Dakota 1987-2005
- John Edwards (2004),[112][113] Senator from North Carolina 1999–2005
- Chuck Hagel (1999, 2000),[114] Senator from Nebraska 1997–2009, Secretary of Defense 2013–2015.
- John Kerry (2012),[3] 68th United States Secretary of State and Senator from Massachusetts (1985–2013)
- Sam Nunn (1996, 1997),[8][better source needed] Senator from Georgia 1972–1997

Governors

- Mitchell Daniels (2012)[115] Governor of Indiana 2004–2013
- Jon Huntsman, Jr. (2012),[3] Governor of Utah 2005–2009
- Rick Perry (2007),[116] Governor of Texas 2000–2015
- Mark Sanford (2008),[117] Governor of South Carolina 2003–2011
- Kathleen Sebelius (2008),[2] Governor of Kansas 2003-2009

United States Military

- Lyman Lemnitzer (1963),[26] Supreme Allied Commander NATO 1963–1969 (deceased)
- Alexander Haig (1978),[72] NATO Commander 1974–1979 (US Secretary of State 1981–1982) (deceased)
- Keith B. Alexander (2012),[3] Commander US Cyber Command; Director, National Security Agency.
- David Petraeus (2013), former Director of the Central Intelligence Agency

Belgium

- King Philippe of Belgium (2007–2009, 2012)[1][2][3]

Commonwealth realms

- Prince Charles, Prince of Wales, Commonwealth realms (1986)[4][5]
- Prince Phillip, Duke of Edinburgh, Commonwealth realms (1965, 1967)[6][7]

Netherlands

- Queen Beatrix of the Netherlands (1997, 2000, 2006, 2008–2015)[8][*better source needed*][3][9][10][11][12][13][14]
- Prince Bernhard of the Netherlands (1954–1975)[15][16] (deceased)
- Willem-Alexander of the Netherlands (2008)[2]

Norway

- King Harald V of Norway[17] (1984[18])
- Haakon, Crown Prince of Norway (2011)[19]

Spain

- Juan Carlos I of Spain, King of Spain (2004)[20]
- Queen Sofía of Spain (2008–2011)[10][11][21]

Austria

- <u>Werner Faymann</u> (2009,[22] 2011,[11] 2012[3])
  Chancellor 2008–present
- <u>Heinz Fischer</u> (2010,[23] 2015[24]) Federal President
  2004–present
- <u>Alfred Gusenbauer</u> (2007,[25] 2015[24]) Chancellor
  2007–2008

Belgium

- <u>Herman Van Rompuy</u>, President of the <u>European
  Council</u>
- <u>Paul-Henri Spaak</u>, Former Prime Minister and
  Secretary General of NATO[26] (1963) (deceased)

Bulgaria

- <u>Nikolai Kamov</u>, Member of Parliament[27] (1999)

Canada

- <u>Mike Harris</u>, (2006),[28] <u>Premier of Ontario</u> 1995–
  2002
- <u>Bernard Lord</u>, (2006),[28] <u>Premier of New Brunswick</u>
  1999–2006
- <u>Gordon Campbell</u>, (2010),[23] <u>Premier of British
  Columbia</u> 2001–2011
- <u>Nigel S. Wright</u>, (2012)[29] <u>Chief of Staff</u>, <u>Office of the
  Prime Minister of Canada</u>, 2011–2013
- <u>Alison Redford</u>, (2012),[3] <u>Premier of Alberta</u> 2011-
  2014

- Frank McKenna, (2006, 2008, 2010, 2012, 2013)[30] Premier of New Brunswick 1987-1997
- Brad Wall, (2013[12]) Premier of Saskatchewan 2007–current

Prime Ministers

- Lester B. Pearson, (1968),[31] Prime Minister of Canada (1963–1968)(deceased)
- Pierre Elliott Trudeau, (1968),[28] Prime Minister of Canada, 1968–1979, 1980–1984 (deceased)
- Jean Chrétien, (1996),[32] Prime Minister of Canada, 1993–2003
- Paul Martin, (1996),[32] Prime Minister of Canada, 2003–2006
- Stephen Harper, (2003),[28] Prime Minister of Canada, 2006–2015

China

- Fu Ying (2011, 2012),[31][33] Vice-Minister of Foreign Affairs, former Ambassador to the UK and Australia

Finland

- Eero Heinäluoma (2006),[34] former chairman of the Social Democratic Party, Minister of Finance 2005-2007
- Jyrki Katainen (2007, 2009),[35][36][37] chairman of the National Coalition Party, former Minister of Finance and current Prime Minister

- Sauli Niinistö (1997),[8][better source needed] former Minister of Finance, former Speaker of the Parliament, current President of the Republic
- Alexander Stubb (2015[38]), Minister of Finance, chairman of the National Coalition Party, former Prime Minister
- Jutta Urpilainen (2012,[39] 2013[12]), former Minister of Finance
- Matti Vanhanen (2009),[36][37] former Prime Minister, former chairman of Centre Party

France

- Gaston Defferre (1964),[40] member of National Assembly and mayor of Marseille (at the time) (deceased)
- Christine Lagarde (2013[12]), Minister of Finance 2007-2011, Managing Director of the International Monetary Fund 2011-
- Georges Pompidou, Prime Minister of France 1962-1968, President of the French Republic 1969-1974[41] (deceased)

Germany

- Guido Westerwelle (2007),[42] Chairman of the Free Democratic Party of Germany and Minister of Foreign Affairs of Germany.
- Helmut Schmidt, West German Chancellor[15]
- Angela Merkel (2005), German Chancellor[43]
- Joschka Fischer (2008), Foreign Minister 1998-2005[43]

- Peer Steinbrück (2011), German Chancellor Candidate[44]
- Jürgen Trittin (2012), Environment Minister 1998-2005[43]

Greece

- George Alogoskoufis (2008, 2009), Minister of Economy and Finance 2004-2009[2][45]
- Dora Bakoyannis (2009), Minister for Foreign Affairs 2006-2009[45]
- Anna Diamantopoulou (2008, 2009), Member of Parliament[2][45]
- Anastasios Giannitsis (2012), Minister of the Interior (Greece) 2011-2012[3]
- Giorgos Papakonstantinou (2010, 2011), Minister of Finance 2009-2011[11][23]
- Yannis Papathanasiou (2009), Minister for Economy and Finance 2009[45]
- Yannis Stournaras (2009), Minister of Finance 2012-2013[45]

Iceland

- Bjarni Benediktsson[46] (1965, 1967, 1970),[47] Mayor of Reykjavík 1940–47, Foreign Minister 1947–55, editor of *The Morning Paper* 1956–59, Minister of Justice and Ecclesiastical Affairs 1959–63, Prime Minister 1963–70 (deceased)
- Björn Bjarnason[46] (1974, 1977),[48] Assistant editor of *The Morning Paper* 1984–1991, Minister of Education 1995–2002, Minister of Justice and Ecclesiastical Affairs 2003, 2009

- Davíð Oddsson[46] (*ca.* 1991–1999), Mayor of Reykjavík 1982–1991, Prime Minister 1991–2004, Foreign Minister 2004–2005, Central Bank governor 2005–2009, editor of *The Morning Paper* as of September 2009
- Einar Benediktsson[46] (*ca.* 1970), ambassador: OECD 1956–60, UK 1982–1986, European Union *et al.* 1986–1991, NATO 1986–1990, United States *et al.* 1993–1997, *etc.*[49]
- Geir Haarde,[50] Central Bank economist 1977–1983, member and chairman of the Parliament's Foreign Affairs Committee 1991–1998, Minister of Finance 1998–2005, Foreign Minister 2005–2006, Prime Minister 2006–2009
- Geir Hallgrímsson[46] (*ca.* 1974–1977,[48][51] 1980[52]), Mayor of Reykjavík 1959–72, Prime Minister 1974–1978, Foreign Minister 1983–1986, Central Bank governor 1986–1990 (deceased)
- Jón Sigurðsson[46] (1993), IMF Board of Directors 1974–1987, Minister of Justice and Ecclesiastical Affairs 1987–88, Industry and Commerce 1988–93, Central Bank governor 1993–94, Nordic Investment Bank governor 1994–2005[53]

Ireland

- Garret FitzGerald (1985), former Taoiseach (deceased)[54]
- Paul Gallagher, Attorney General of Ireland[23][54]
- Dermot Gleeson, former Attorney General of Ireland[45]
- Charlie McCreevy[54]

- Michael McDowell (2007), former Attorney General, former Minister for Justice, Equality and Law Reform[1][54]
- Michael Noonan, (2012), then Minister for Finance.[54][55]
- Peter Sutherland, Director General of the WTO and former Attorney General of Ireland[54]
- Simon Coveney, (2014), then Minister for Agriculture, Food and the Marine, shortly afterwards became Minister for Defence[29][56]

Italy

- Enrico Letta, former Prime Minister
- Emma Bonino, former Minister of Foreign Affairs
- Mario Draghi, President of the European Central Bank
- Mario Monti, Economist,[32] former Prime Minister
- Renato Ruggiero, former WTO director, politician[32]

Japan

- Nobuo Tanaka (2009), Executive Director of the International Energy Agency 2007-2011[45]

Netherlands

- Ruud Lubbers, Prime Minister 1982-1994[41]
- Wim Kok, Prime Minister 1994-2002[41]
- Jan-Peter Balkenende (2008), Prime Minister 2002-2010[2][41]
- Maxime Verhagen, Minister[41]
- Mark Rutte, the current Prime Minister[57]

- Alexander Pechtold, leader of D66, a political party[57]

Norway

- Jens Stoltenberg (2002),the former Prime Minister of Norway.[17]
- Kristin Clemet[17] (1999, 2008[58]) Managing Director of the liberal and conservative think tank Civita, Former Minister of Education and Science.
- Geir Lundestad (2005)[59] Director of the Norwegian Nobel institute and Secretary to The Nobel Peace Prize Committee.

Poland

- Józef Retinger (1954 to 1960), Founder and secretary of Bilderberg Group[16][60] (deceased)
- Andrzej Olechowski (1994, 2004, 2005)[61]
- Hanna Suchocka (1998)
- Jan Vincent-Rostowski (2012)[29]

Portugal

- António José Seguro, Politician[62]
- Paulo Portas, Politician[62]
- Luís Amado, Politician[62]
- Paulo Rangel, Politician[62]
- Francisco Pinto Balsemão (1981, 1983–1985, 1987–2008),[1] former Prime Minister of Portugal, 1981–1983 and CEO of Impresa media group
- Manuel Pinho (2009),[63][64] former Minister of Economy and Innovation

- José Sócrates (2004),[63][64][65] former Prime Minister of Portugal
- José Pedro Aguiar-Branco,[63][64][65] former Minister of Justice
- Santana Lopes (2004),[63][64][65] former Prime Minister of Portugal
- José Manuel Durão Barroso (1994, 2003, 2005, 2013),[12][63][66][67] former Prime Minister of Portugal and Minister of Foreign Affairs, and current President of the European Commission
- Nuno Morais Sarmento,[64][65] former Minister of Presidency and Minister of Parliament Affairs
- António Costa (2008),[64][65] former Minister of Interior and current Mayor of Lisbon
- Rui Rio (2008),[64][65] former Mayor of Porto
- Manuela Ferreira Leite (2009),[64][68] former Minister of Education and Minister of Finance and Public Administration
- Augusto Santos Silva,[64] former Minister of Education, Minister of Culture, Minister of Parliament Affairs, and current Minister of National Defence
- Marcelo Rebelo de Sousa (1998),[64] former Minister of Parliament Affairs
- António Guterres (1994),[64][66][67] former Prime Minister of Portugal, former President of the Socialist International and current United Nations High Commissioner for Refugees
- Ferro Rodrigues,[66] former Minister of Labour and Social Solidarity and Minister of Public Works, Transport and Communications
- Jorge Sampaio,[66][67] former President of Portugal
- Luís Mira Amaral (1995),[67][69] former Minister of Labour and Social Solidarity, chairman of Caixa

Geral de Depósitos and CEO of Banco Português de Investimento

- Vítor Constâncio (1988),[67][69] governor of the Banco de Portugal, Vice President of the ECB
- Fernando Teixeira dos Santos (2010),[69] former Minister of Finance
- José Medeiros Ferreira (1977, 1980),[69] former Minister of Foreign Affairs
- Joaquim Ferreira do Amaral (1999),[69] former Minister of Public Works, Transport and Communications
- António Miguel Morais Barreto (1992),[69] former Minister of Agriculture, Rural Development and Fisheries
- João Cravinho,[70] former Minister for Environment, Spatial Planning and Regional Development
- Artur Santos Silva,[70] former vice-governor of the Banco de Portugal, chairman of Banco Português de Investimento and current non-executive chairman of Jerónimo Martins
- Francisco Luís Murteira Nabo,[70] former chairman of Portugal Telecom, Minister of Public Works, Transport and Communications, and current chairman of Galp Energia and president of the Portuguese Economists Association

Spain

- María Dolores de Cospedal (2011), Secretary General of the People's Party[11]
- Bernardino León Gross (2008, 2010, 2011), Secretary General of Office of the Prime Minister[2][11][23]

- Miguel Ángel Moratinos (2009), <u>Minister of Foreign Affairs</u> 2004-2010[45]
- Soraya Sáenz de Santamaría (2012), <u>Deputy Prime Minister</u>[3]
- Pedro Solbes (2009), <u>Minister of Economy and Finance</u> 1993-1996, 2004-2009[45]
- José Luis Rodríguez Zapatero (2010), Prime Minister 2004–2011[23]

Sweden

- Carl Bildt (2006,[71] 2008,[71] 2009, 2013[12]) Prime Minister 1991–1994, Minister of Foreign Affairs 2006–2014
- Anders Borg (2007,[71] 2013[12]) Minister of Finance 2006–2014
- Thorbjörn Fälldin (1978),[72] Prime Minister 1976–1978
- Maud Olofsson (2008),[71] Minister of Industry 2006–2011
- Fredrik Reinfeldt (2006),[71] Prime Minister 2006–2014
- Mona Sahlin (1996),[71] Head of the Swedish social democratic party 2007–2011

Switzerland

- Christoph Blocher (2009),[45] former Member of <u>Federal Council</u> and former CEO of EMS Group
- Doris Leuthard (2011),[11] Member of <u>Federal Council</u>
- Rolf Schweiger (2011)[73]

Turkey

- Ali Babacan (2003, 2004, 2005, 2007, 2008, 2009, 2012, 2013), Minister of Economic Affairs 2002-2007, Minister of Foreign Affairs 2007-2009, Deputy Prime Minister 2009-2015[2][3][12][45]

United Kingdom

- Shirley Williams (at least 2010, 2013[12]), stateswoman and member, House of Lords; Harvard University Professor; Past President, Chatham House; int'l member, Council on Foreign Relations.[74]
- Paddy Ashdown (1989),[75] former leader of Liberal Democrats, High Representative for Bosnia and Herzegovina
- Ed Balls (2006),[76] former Economic Secretary to the Treasury and advisor to British Prime Minister Gordon Brown and was Secretary of State for Children, Schools and Families (2007–2010)
- Peter Carington, 6th Baron Carrington (Steering Committee member),[77] former Foreign Secretary
- Kenneth Clarke (1993,[78] 1998,[79] 1999,[80] 2003,[81] 2004,[82] 2006,[83] 2007,[83] 2008,[84][85] 2013[12]) Chancellor of the Exchequer 1993–1997, Shadow Secretary of State for Business, Enterprise and Regulatory Reform 2008–2010, Lord Chancellor, Secretary of State for Justice 2010–2012, Minister without Portfolio 2012–current
- Robert Gascoyne-Cecil (Viscount Cranborne) (1997),[8][better source needed] Leader of the House of Lords 1994–1997

- Denis Arthur Greenhill, Lord Greenhill of Harrow (deceased) (1974),[86]) former Head of Foreign and Commonwealth Office
- Denis Healey (founder and Steering Committee member),[77] former Chancellor of the Exchequer (deceased)
- John Kerr (2008–2013, 2015),[2][3][11][12][14][23][45] member of the House of Lords and Deputy Chairman of Royal Dutch Shell
- Peter Mandelson (1999,[87] 2008,[2] 2009,[88] 2011–2013[3][11][12]) Business Secretary (2008–2010)
- John Monks (1996),[32] former TUC General Secretary
- George Osborne (2006,[89] 2007,[89] 2008[90] 2009,[91] 2013[12]) Shadow Chancellor of the Exchequer (2004–2010), Chancellor of the Exchequer 2010–current
- David Owen (1982),[92] former British Foreign Secretary and leader of the Social Democratic Party
- Enoch Powell, (deceased) (1968),[93] MP and Ulster Unionist
- Malcolm Rifkind (1996),[32] former Foreign Secretary
- Eric Roll (1964, 1966, 1967, 1973–1975, 1977–1999) (Bilderberg Steering Committee),[94] Department of Economic Affairs, 1964, later Bilderberg Group Chairman (deceased)
- David Hannay, Baron Hannay of Chiswick (1995),[95] Diplomatic posts at European Union and United Nations.
- John Smith (1989) (deceased),[96] Labour Party leader

Prime Ministers

- <u>Tony Blair</u> (1993),[78][97] Prime Minister 1997–2007
- <u>Gordon Brown</u> (1991),[98] Prime Minister 2007– 2010
- <u>Edward Heath</u>,[15] Prime Minister 1970–1974 (deceased)
- <u>Alec Douglas-Home</u> (1977–1980),[99] Chairman of the Bilderberg Group, Prime Minister 1963–1964 (deceased)
- <u>Margaret Thatcher</u> (at least 1975, 1977, 1986),[100][101][102] Prime Minister 1979–1990 (deceased)
- <u>David Cameron</u> (2013) Currently Prime Minister

These are the names of those from other countries, they're from all over the world, Kings, Queens, Princes, Chancellors, Prime Ministers, and more.

As you can see they are from Belgium, Commonwealth realms, Netherlands, Norway, Spain, Austria, Bulgaria, Canada, China, Finland, France, Germany Greece, Iceland, Ireland, Italy, Japan, Poland, Portugal, Sweden, Switzerland, Turkey, and many more countries including United Kingdom.

All we really know about the group is that they are very important powerful and wealthy people who meet in secret. Why is it so secret, what is it that they do not wish to share with the rest of us? Do they have a plan for the rest of us? Could they be the ones our Presidents have talked about when they speak of the New World Order?

Is it not a concern when we have David Petraeus, former CIA Director, John Kerry 68th United States Secretary of State, Hillary R. Clinton Former First Lady, Former Secretary of State and current Presidential candidate, George H.W. Bush, Bill Clinton, and Gerald Ford all Former Presidents?

Are we not to question when our leaders of high position go into a secret meeting with other countries and bankers? Is this not a conflict of interests? Why are not all Presidents invited? Where is the check and balance system at, when the doors are closed on those we wish to check? Hillary Rodham Clinton has already been proven to be deceitful from undergoing sniper fire, Benghazi, and the current E-mail scandal.

Chemtrails, Death from above

Let us look at one more conspiracy, chemtrails, here we end the book as we look not across the states, but up, high in the sky where no shadows of deception should be found, yet still are.

Trails that appear behind planes and then disappear then back again, for no apparent reason. Is this something that is being turned on and off from above? Trails that appear black as you watch planes follow these trails and release a chemical spray that is visible to the eye. Trails that loop with no true sense of direction. They use the defense it is because of weather modification, or to protect us from global warming, and to save us from the terrorists.

They mention in case there is a biological attack from the terrorists that these training exercises will save us, really? Why not build the wall and protect our borders and prevent our country from becoming a battlefield.

They show a chemical after it had fallen from above on a fence. The chemical appears almost like a cobweb. Our military once again admits to using chemical weapons tests. They talk about short term exposure where there are symptoms of stomach to chest pains. Long term exposure causes, or can cause blood pressure problems.

They talk about Chemtrail researchers mentioning that it could be used to wear down a person's immune system. If they have Chemtrail researchers than it must be authentic, maybe we need to pay closer attention to this.

Is this a game of chess?

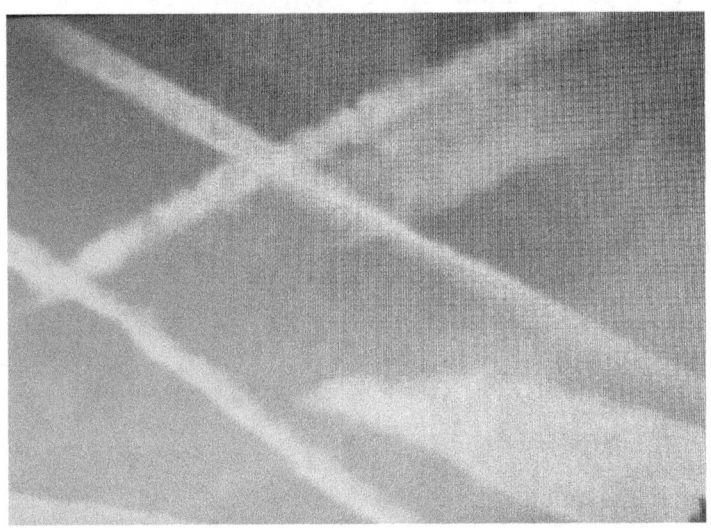

Are we the pawns that are waiting for the next move, or will they simply say check mate?

The famous singer and showman Prince encouraged the audience where he was talking at to investigate Chemtrails. He stated he first learned of them from Dick Gregory, a civil rights leader, during the State of the Black Union speech. He mentioned growing up looking at them thinking they looked pretty neat, then you all of a sudden noticed more and more of them and people fighting. There were no real reasons why they were fighting, they just were.

They state the United States Government has a long history of testing biological and chemical agents on the unknowing public.

In 1977 the United States Army declassified hundreds of pages of documents titled, The U.S. Army activity in the US biological warfare program. It showed 249 populated areas that were contaminated with biological agents between 1949 and 1969 by the United States Army secret testing program.

There was **Project Shad** (shipboard hazard in defense) It was used to expose military personnel to biological and chemical agents without their knowledge.

Weather modifications is another area that has been brought up. All the way back to the 1950's, governments were experimenting with weather conditions and doing so successfully, manipulating weather patterns.

The British government had a program called **Project cumulous**. It was a cloud seeding and testing program that created excessive rain to slow the movement of their enemy.

The United States was involved with one as well called **Project Popeye,** used during the Vietnam war which was cloud seeding, and used for the same purpose.

China admitted to using it to clear the smog out of the air for a parade celebrating their 60th anniversary of communist in China.

Is there nothing sacred or real anymore? Are we living in a world built on deception? As we head into the conclusion of this book, keep an open mind to both sides and remember what means nothing today may mean everything tomorrow.

CONCLUSION

We have traveled through the pages of Deception starting out East, with the Sandy Hook conspiracy, where the characters appear created, or implausible at that. Where children have not only died once, but twice in other countries. Where the entire crime scene seemed staged and rehearsed, with actors walking routes, children photographed coming out of the school twice, and law enforcement there ahead of the call.

The media focused on the guns rather than the shooter. The families of the victims cries were tearless, the shooters family, still a mystery. All this created to sell the American people on gun control. The question is, how much is real and how much is not?

When you look at the event and know the President of the United States goal, is more gun control. When you know our Commander in Chief is more focused on protecting the Muslim community, rather than the American interests as a whole makes you wonder.

Seems not everyone made the photo?

We now move on, as we travel to the Southern States, where questions of our military's use of force in our civilian occupied territory is challenged, with Jade Helm. Where military officers justify their operations by informing us that it is strictly for the purpose of training soldiers to the different types of terrains. Where they show States on a map as friendly or unfriendly.

Others believe that it is a ruse to get Americans accustomed to seeing large amounts of military personnel in our civilian populated communities. We see Jade II as more than just science, but rather a covert operation by those that secretly want to run our country by gathering large amounts of information that will someday be used against us, making us slaves of our own doing.

Jade Helm a civil war in the making?

The soldiers that are our Sons and Daughters will they then become our enemy?

As we head back to New York, we look at 9/11 as one of Americas most horrific events, one that has forever scared our country and made us feel vulnerable. As we watch in devastation as towers come collapsing down with such precision as to create suspicion and doubt.

Where experts in the engineering field, along with Architectural experts disagree with the evidence that our White House Spokesmen, and political committees, along with the National Institute of Standards and Technology show. The NIST refused to validate their findings by choice, adding more speculation and doubt.

We have four planes that appear to be destroyed, at one time yet two are shown still in flight. AKARS DATA, a device used to communicate with aircraft, shows UA175 still airborne in Western Pennsylvania. This was approximately twenty minutes after the reported crash.

This was the one time that Firemen and Police Officers were seen as heroes.

Sad that it would take a tragedy to make us look at them as anything but what they have always been.

We visited Texas as we discussed Waco a community destroyed for one man, David Koresh, by the heavily armed ATF. Much of the assault seemed like over kill as dogs were killed vehicles crushed by tanks and a building where all exits were destroyed to prevent escapes and the chance of any survivors coming out alive, or as witnesses. Where the negotiator tells the Branch Davidians to stay inside or suffer the consequences.

Here the children didn't appear to matter as they did in Connecticut, maybe because these children were for guns, rather than against.

As we stay here in the South in Oklahoma we again see America under attack, yet those that are the targets seem to not be in range? It appears again as our investigative abilities get better the more questions arise of things that don't add up. A Federal building where the ATF were tipped off and none present during the explosion and those that were are said to be lying.

Evidence of more than one person being involved with very detailed descriptions as they then are just forgotten with no explanation. The amount and substance of the explosives continued to change, whether because of new information, or making it a better fit for the information they already had.

As you read and check out all the links I have presented, you can be, not only your own detective, but the judge as you are free to judge this information as fact or fiction. I hope this book at least makes you think about all that we have covered.

Now let's head out to the North West, to the grand State of Idaho. While we may also be traveling further back in time, we are still dreaming of a better future. A man by the name of Randy Weaver catches the eyes of the U.S. Marshals as it is during these times that there are some very radical groups that do need to be watched.

This event though while separate than the one in Texas called Waco had a lot of similarities. There was just one man that was wanted by the Federal government agency. There were lots of law enforcement brought in with heavy military tanks. Both events became televised standoffs, and it appears both were cover ups.

The question is did they learn from Ruby Ridge not to have survivors where they may have to pay them a large amount of money in a civil suit? I in no way am siding with those that break the law, but just want the truth to be presented and let justice do what it was intended to do judge fairly.

You can see we have traveled around this country in this book but it is time to head back East to Boston, as we look at the Boston Marathon bombing.

Warnings are posted everywhere right off the starting line as FBI agents are seen all over, with Bomb sniffing dogs and supposedly bomb exercises going on in the very area that a major publicized event was about to take place.

Then there is, none other than Carlos Arredondo an illegal or not so illegal. At the beginning of the video you see Carlos with another gentleman holding up a sign that says, (Latinos remaking America). He is seen as a hero. Why? He is seen on video helping push a victim in a wheelchair, but the closer you watch the more he appears to be one of those crisis actors as he keeps changing ID's, and video shows his statements to be false and inaccurate, along with his strange behavior focusing on the flag rather than the crisis.

Is he a hero because he is Mexican, or Latino and he is remaking America? Who is he remaking it for, the New World Order?

Let's look at another event that happened in Belgium, an explosion that injured Mason Wells, who is 19 years old. What makes this so interesting is he is only 19 and has already traveled to two places where bombs had exploded making him a very unlucky guy. To me adds more doubt that now this event is even real, after all we are seeing patterns of people that appear to be the same people all over these big crisis.

Where there is smoke there is usually fire. Even our news agencies try to persuade us through deception as they have been caught trying to trick us in their real locations, why? What is their true objective? Are they trying to inform us, or direct us and for whom, or what? Maybe it is all for entertainment purposes.

As we come to the end we have to look at everything, for no information withheld is entirely useless.

We will head back to Texas, where everything is bigger including its secrets. The biggest or most famous conspiracy for many will be the assassination of President John F. Kennedy. This was at that time, an event that shocked the world, but even to this day the event is clouded in mystery with angles and ballistics, and the mysterious umbrella man and the braking of the driver, while in a fire fight.

Now this year brings yet another death clouded in mystery as Justice Scalia dies and is suddenly declared dead by normal causes, before even being seen. Rumors of scandals are brought to life as our Presidential candidates fight to be the next Commander in Chief. President Obama is livid on getting his own people properly placed in the White House, including a new Supreme Court Justice that thinks their way, or what I call a yes man on the Democratic side.

Just look at how the RNC has pushed Donald Trump to promise not to run against the Republican Party if he loses, as an Independent. The problem is he is not getting the same cooperativeness back, meaning they are purposely trying to ambush him with everything they have. He is the only candidate that has spoke freely for the American people, while not being worried to offend the establishment. Ted Cruz and Governor Kasich are the only other two that should be considered for the Presidential candidacy, but watch what is going to happen. I predict this year's election is going to be monumental.

Thank you for traveling with me through this book exploring the conspiracies that have been created by all the colorful actors, and politicians. I can say that what we have covered in this book does bring chills to me. The links are all there to be viewed at your convenience and discretion.

I love my country and I love God I think as Americans we are suppose to love them both and protect them both. As we raise our hand and swear on the bible in court, why have our leaders who swore the same oath not fought harder for the Bible? Why does the New World Order always appear as though it is the almighty?

The following information is protected Under section 107 of the Copy Right Act of 1976, where allowance is made for fair use, for the purpose of criticism, comments, news reporting, teaching, scholarship and research.

I wish to end this book on one note. That America has been constantly changing, it is up to all of us to make our country great again. Remember when you vote it is not about Democrat or Republican, it is about America and Americans.

ABOUT THE AUTHOR

Timothy J. Amdahl grew up in a small town, called Estherville, Iowa. He graduated in 1981 and served two years with the Army and then transferred in to the United States Marine Corps. He was honorably discharged in 1987 after serving four and a half years in the Marine Corps. He has worked as a youth counselor for four years helping the children of our future.

He is married with four children and is currently working for the Illinois Department of Corrections as a Correctional officer, having already served fourteen years. He is a proud American who only wishes to unite our country once again in these troubling times.

Changing America is focused on bringing out concerns and challenging all of us on keeping our government honest and Americans safe with the hope our country can once again prosper. You need me and I need you, let's make America great again Let us pick the next President of the United States.

www.ingramcontent.com/pod-product-compliance
Lightning Source LLC
Chambersburg PA
CBHW071342280526
45787CB00001B/181